Memories of a Lost World
Adventures Far Off the Beaten Path in the 1980's and 1990's
Volume Two

Thomas H Murray

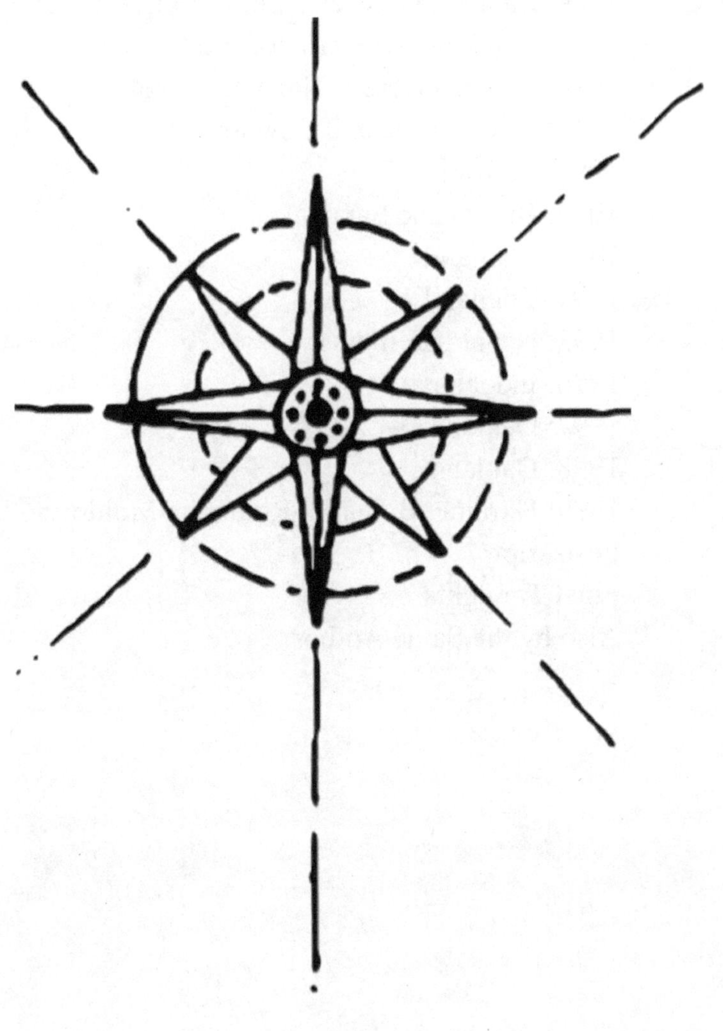

TABLE OF CONTENTS

Introduction	4
Preface	8
1988: Burma and Japan	11
1989: Bahrain, Greece, Turkey, Yugoslavia, Austria, Switzerland, and France	33
1990: Arizona Desert, North Carolina Mountains, and Cowboy Texas	67
1991: Taiwan	75
1992: Brunei and Sarawak	91
1993: Thailand	98
1994: Thailand	113
1995: Nepal and India	137
1996: Indochina	169
1997: Oakland	201
1998: Oakland	218
1999: Ukraine, Bulgaria, Romania, Moldova	238
Postscript	260
Final Thoughts	261
Also by the Same Author	262

INTRODUCTION

There was a time, long before cell phones, virtual reality, and the internet, when the world was a bigger place. To experience the world, one had to leave the comfort zone of one's home and physically travel across oceans, mountains, and other relatively unknown expanses. One had to cross borders to learn about other cultures, histories, and languages. The old recluse of the reclusives, books, even National Geographic and TV documentaries could help. But all of those were mere snippets of the full kaleidoscope of experiences touching all our five senses that being there would offer.

I was a very unusual product of my country. Though I grew up in a racist society, I could never understand it. Instead of being put off by the 'other', I was very attracted to anyone who was different from me. That included race, religion, country of origin, etc. I had the simple-minded belief that I could learn from those who are different. Someone of another race had a unique life experience. Those of other religions had a different outlook on reality. As for foreigners who spoke with an accent, they represented a whole different world of culture and language.

In third grade, I befriended the only African American student in my class. He spent many weekends in my cookie cutter suburban home. His home, however, was like a different planet. In a large old house hidden down in the small forest and thickets below a busy intersection was a large extended family of many generations: uncles, aunts, grandparents, cousins, siblings, etc. I had passed through that intersection many times, never realizing the world waiting below. I remember opossums hanging to dry from a tree branch. Old black potbellied stoves to heat the rooms in the Pennsylvania winters. Six or more of us children sleeping in an enormous bed, watching old horror films on a big black-and-white TV before falling asleep together.

I caught a lot of heat in high school when I befriended the few African American classmates we had. My best friend, may he rest in peace, was a quiet, well-mannered, very intelligent African American. I spent weekends at his home and he at mine. We went to my family's Episcopal church near Annapolis one weekend, and the church was scandalized that I brought him. I had been to his Methodist church, which welcomed me. I was scandalized that they served grape juice in little plastic cups for Communion.

While in high school, I started my lifetime interest in all things Chinese and Asian. This led me to the University of Chicago, which had the best Asian studies and Chinese language program in the country. From there it was just a matter of time before I decided that I needed to see not just China, or Asia, but the entire world. My lifetime goal was to visit every country in the world, every single one.

At the age of twenty, after two years of intensive Mandarin studies, I enrolled in Fu Ren University in Taiwan to study Mandarin. China was not yet open to foreign students. I had about four months of free time. So, I embarked on my dream to experience the world directly. My first stop was in the opposite direction, to visit old Mother Britain, then as much of Europe as four months would allow.

This is also an account of me as revealed in actions, thoughts, and attitudes as a young man. I was twenty when I started my world travels. The reader can track the changes as a youth slowly became a man. The reader can see what my base values were, which have never changed. Originally, I wanted to name this book, "A Portrait of the Author as a Young Man". Later, I thought that would be somewhat pretentious, as some may catch the reference to James

Joyce's famous work, "A Portrait of the Artist as a Young Man". Nonetheless, this work reflects the sentiment of that title.

Except for Western Europe, there were few Americans from the US backpacking around the world. In Europe, they followed the well-worn trail as paved by 'Let's Go Europe', a guidebook that tried to give brief advice on what to see, where to stay and eat, and how to get around for every country on the western side of the Iron Curtain. Otherwise, most Americans from the US I met were on a mission, either in the military or as missionaries.

We all were born somewhere from two individuals whom we call our parents. As for the where, I was born in Philadelphia on the east coast of the US. Most importantly, my parents influenced me at an early age, which molded my childhood thinking and attitudes. They shaped me into my early teens, and I took it from there.

My mother gave me a passion for culture, history, and foreign languages. She took the time to share with me all the major operas at the Philadelphia Opera, the great tradition of fine art at the Philadelphia Museum of Art, trips to all the historic sites within a few hours' drive, including Valley Forge, Gettysburg, the Liberty Bell, etc. Our home was filled with books of literature and poetry. She taught me French as a child and allowed me to learn how to sing and play the piano, violin, clarinet, among others.

My father had different interests than hers, mainly involving racing cars, bicycles, and motorcycles. Besides forming my character, the main responsibility of fathers to their sons, he gave me something which may appear small in comparison but turns out to be of primary importance. As a child, I often heard him recount experiences as stories from various episodes in his life. They may seem quite minor to me now, but not so then. Whenever he told a story to a gathering of his friends, I always was very impressed. I silently wished that one day I, too, could recount interesting stories of my life experiences to others. Of course, that required me to live an interesting life, which has compelled me to live the life I have and still do. And that, dear readers, is what this book is about.

Preface

It already has been over forty years since I took that cheap charter flight from Newark Airport to London's Gatwick. Over these decades and eighty-nine countries later, occasionally someone would say something at the dinner party table that would spark a random memory from one of my adventures traveling. It might be something like when I came under mortar attack by bandits in Laos, or directly experiencing the guerilla war struggle in the Philippines, or visiting the opium cultivating hill tribes far outside the control of the Thai government, or crossing the Soviet Union on the Trans-Siberian railroad, a cobra knocking pans to my kitchen floor in Taiwan, or the fervor of the Tibetan pilgrims in Lhasa, etc. Invariably someone would say, "You really ought to write a book."

First, I thought that I could do so once I stop traveling, still many decades into the future. But would my mind be clear and, more importantly, would my memory serve me well enough to reconstruct my experiences and adventures?

Then, I thought who would be interested in my travel logs in the world of non-stop travel blogs and everything else that fills the ether of the internet? Maybe a blog would be more interesting to the present generation than the antique technology of a book. Quickly reaching the age of antiquehood, I decided to stick with what I know best. But the world is full of travel adventures. Surely, we do not need yet another.

In the end, I decided that I did indeed have something most people do not have today. I have memories of adventures at a time when the world was a very different place. Besides the total lack of basic technologies that we take for granted today, the Cold War was in full swing. The world was divided into two distinct camps, led by the US and the Soviet Union. Most governments, in what we used to call the Third World, did not have control of extensive areas outside of the central cultural zones. Various guerrilla movements or simply bandits controlled many of these regions. These memories start in the depths of the Cold War and extend beyond the collapse of the Soviet Union, from 1983 to 1999.

For a typical journey, I planned on six or seven months to step outside whatever comfort zone I was living in at the time and map out a route that crossed many borders. I traveled overland, which sometimes would put me in areas where, in hindsight, I probably should never have gone. But danger meant little to me then.

The verb 'to backpack' was very important to me. In the early years, I carried a sleeping bag strapped to the bottom of my backpack. I slept in parks, under trees, on beaches, in the back of lorries, on the floor of slow night trains, etc. Of course, I was a young man in my early twenties.

Very often people would ask me, "Ah, wonderful. I wish I had the money to travel." My reply was the same as it was truthful. Traveling like I did for that amount of time, including airfare to get there, etc. all in, was less than my living expenses wherever was serving as my base. In Asia, I routinely did not spend over ten US dollars a day, including airfare, local transportation, eating, sleeping, etc. I spent only twice that in Europe.

So, for 300 to 600 US dollars a month, I could travel as freely as I wished. Or for three times that amount, I could be anchored in one place, 'getting things done'. The people telling me that were spending much more per month than me. I was not seeing the world. I was experiencing the world with all five senses. They, on the other hand, were 'getting things done' working in a career that allowed them the golden anchors of houses, cars, family, and career.

It is all about priorities. The irony is that after I started 'getting serious things done' and entered my career, I more than surpassed them with material trappings. The difference is the time I took to experience the world and take the risks of a young man has made me who I am today. My knowledge of humankind in a wide range of cultures and contexts has greatly helped me along the myriad paths of life.

Dedications

I dedicate this book of memories to all the multitudes of people who touched my life in so many ways from all around the world.

Notes

This is a book of actual experiences. Real people doing real things. The people are safe because I cannot remember their names anyway. Nothing has been changed, except what the fog of time can do to memories. Fortunately, while cleaning out the basement of my house, I discovered three travel journals, which served as my diaries all those decades ago. They have served me well in filling in the foggy blanks that otherwise would have been an obstacle.

Many place names have changed over the years. I used the names as I knew them when I traveled there.

1988

Burma and Japan

Burma 1988

How Far Can a Bottle and a Carton Go?

In the summer of 1987, I tried to visit Burma (Myanmar) from Calcutta but only got as far as Bangladesh. While still in Calcutta, I was told that if I sold a bottle of Johnnie Walker Red Label and a carton of 555 cigarettes on the Burmese black market, I could make enough of the local currency to pay for everything for a two-week trip. When my trip to Burma could not happen (read the chapter about Bangladesh), I flew to Bangkok instead. I managed to sell my whisky and cigarettes to a Dhaka airport employee for a bit more than I paid in the duty-free shop. The reason these two are so popular in Burma is that they are obligatory gifts at weddings.

It was the beginning of June 1988, a year later than my original plan. Not much had changed in Burma. I arrived at the sweltering Rangoon (Yangon) airport with my duty-free Johnie Walker and 555 cigarettes. As I was going through airport Customs, the contents of my duty-free bag caught the attention of the Customs inspector. He bought them from me right there on the inspection line in plain sight. The amount in the local currency, Kyat (pronounced 'chat'), was indeed enough to pay for everything, including a driver and his Toyota pickup truck for two weeks. The official exchange rate was twenty times worse for visitors than reality, as represented by the black market rate.

In Rangoon, I stayed at the British-era colonial hotel, the Strand. There had been some maintenance done over the years since independence in 1948, so it was relatively in good condition. The city itself, however, was very run down by Southeast Asian standards of the time.

Rangoon's Shwedagon Paya, the main Buddhist temple of the country with its huge, towering golden dome, was indeed very impressive. At 112 meters (367 feet) tall, sitting on a 51-meter (167 feet) hill, it dominates the skyline. Zoning laws prevent any building from being over 75% of the temple's total height.

The next morning, I awoke at 0400 to start my trip north. My first destination was Pegu (Bago), fifteen hours away. The driver had to pay bribes at the many roadblocks along the way, but the amounts were trivial compared to what I was paying him.

It is the site of the old capital of Pegan which unified much of what is currently Burma and lasted from the 9th to the 13th centuries. It collapsed after the last sacking by the Mongols in 1287. This UNESCO site originally had over 10,000 Buddhist temples in and around the city. 'Only' 2,000 remain as ruins. The once great center of one of the most important empires of Southeast Asia was only scattered remains covered by tall grass.

Sitting on a hill, the view of the widely scattered remains of the white pagodas and palaces was surreal. A horse cart took me around the ruins. Children often tried to sell me gems found in the local rivers. I was not in the gem business. Though ironically decades later I would be. Burma is a major world supplier of a wide range of various gems stones, especially rich in jade.

Our next destination was nearby Mount Popa. A Buddhist monastery sits on the pinnacle. I climbed all 777 steps up to it. Besides an incredible view of the plains below, I met a white-robed monk whose mother was visiting him. The young man emanated the most incredible feeling of peace and tranquility that affects me to this day whenever I remember that experience.

Mandalay is 600 km (373 miles) north of Pegu on the Irrawaddy River, which flows north to south from the Tibetan mountains to the

Andaman Sea. We broke the trip up by staying at Maymyo at one of the old British hill stations, in an old imperial era bachelors' rest house for an old defunct teak company. I had to watch where I stepped on the rotting wooden floors. As with all the hotels I stayed in Burma, some serious maintenance and modern plumbing would have made these places special.

Arriving half a day later, Mandalay proved to be worth the trip. The name itself always occupied a romantic place in my mind. It reminds me of one of my favorite songs: Bomber's Bay by Echo and the Bunnymen. As with many cities in the interior of the entire region, it had changed little in hundreds of years. All the houses near the river were simple wooden structures on stilts to protect against seasonal flooding.

The river is the heart of the city, serving as a major path of commerce for the entire country. I continued north by riverboat to Min Kun for a day trip. The temples and markets were the most interesting parts. At a community center, we watched the beginning of an all-night dance celebrating the life of Buddha. The dancers were backed by a traditional Burmese orchestra with its classical instruments like the Burmese harp, xylophone, leather drums, diverse types of wooden clappers, oboe-like woodwinds, etc. The music they produced was unworldly, wonderful, but difficult to describe.

Between breaks for the dancers, the orchestra would continue to perform music from the US, like Santana's Black Magic Woman and Madonna's Material Girl. In each case, they made the music their own. They were often better than the originals.

From there, I returned to Rangoon with an overnight stop at Pegu. Throughout the trip, we stopped at various villages for lunch and others to take a break. I experienced Burmese life in the countryside. Once, while eating lunch at a local roadside eatery, I was shocked to see something I had never seen outside the southern states of the US.

It was a chain gang. About twenty convicts were chained together with leg irons, guarded by men with shotguns. The major difference is that the chain gangs in the US one sees by the side of the highways all wear obvious state-issued prison uniforms with work boots. Whereas in Burma they wore tattered rags and were barefoot.

The Burmese have curious driving habits. When going downhill, to save fuel, they turned off the engine and then turned it back on just as the vehicle was approaching the bottom. At night, they drove without headlights on and turned them on only when another vehicle approached, blinding each driver in the process. You know, to save gasoline and the electric charge of the battery.

My driver was a university student in a country where the universities were closed because of social and political unrest and a teachers' strike. He spoke quite good English. Later I learned he had escaped as a refugee to Thailand after the student uprising of August 1988, less than two months after my visit.

Several regional minority groups have been fighting a war for autonomy with the central government for decades with success. They control their regions independently of the government, with sophisticated weapons and well-organized militias. Some examples are the Kachin, the Shan, and the Karen states. Many lesser ethnic groups, like the Muslim Rohingya and others, join in whenever possible.

Burma is a Buddhist country of the Theravada (the smaller wheel) branch. This type of Buddhism is common in Thailand, Sri Lanka, Laos, and Cambodia. In contrast with Mahayana Buddhism (the larger wheel), Theravada adherents mainly focus on their own path of liberation. Karma plays a key role in this.

As I experienced in Thailand, too, everything one does produces good karma or bad. Each person has a balance sheet. At the end of life, the account is tallied. If the good outbalances the bad, then one moves further on the path. If the opposite is the case, then one falls behind.

The dictator Ne Win serves as a great example of this. After decades of various crimes in the name of power, as his life was ebbing away, he realized that he may have a problem with his account balance. So, he literally bought enough good karma to ensure forward progress. A monk advisor gave him a sum to donate to build stupas throughout the country for the glorification of Lord Buddha that would be sure to take care of his deficit problem.

So, the corrupt money he gained served to clean his slate of all his other crimes. The tens of thousands of stupas in ruins everywhere indicate that this is not a modern idea. I must admit that this is not what Buddha had in mind, but it is how it is practiced.

In general, the Burmese are some of my favorite people in the world. They are calm, warm, and friendly, despite living in government-created misery. My bottle of Johnnie Walker and a carton of 555 cigarettes went a long way and gave me an amazing life experience.

Visiting a Sino-Burmese Clan House and Temple

Japan 1988

Living at the Foot of Mt. Fuji

After traveling for six months through China and India, I arrived at Glendale, a suburb of Pheonix, Arizona. This was where the American Graduate School of International Management was located. It was one of the best international business schools in the US. It was better known as Thunderbird, named after the Army Air Force training airbase during the Second World War. The school's founder bought the surplus airbase after the war and started a graduate school to train young Americans of the US to succeed in the new world order. It also represented a new phase in my life, one that started my search for a career path where, ultimately, I found outstanding success.

By the time I arrived there in August 1987, it was already surrounded by a combination of suburbia and desert with every day for six months or more having temperatures over 38 C/100 F. At first, I had to walk everywhere until I bought a cheap used bicycle. I used to run sixteen kms/ten miles in the late afternoon as the temperature fell before returning to swim laps in the school's swimming pool.

Because of its global business focus, students had to learn a foreign language. I passed the exams for French and Mandarin. I also passed the placement exams for many of the required basic business classes. This was wonderful, as I could then concentrate on the more interesting elective classes. Accounting was a class that I just had to do, and for two semesters. At first, I was leery of such a boring subject. But thanks to the excellent teacher, I enjoyed it. After all, accounting catches every heartbeat of a company. Statistics proved as boring as I feared. Though I learned that there are three kinds of lies: lies, damn lies, and statistics.

Because of my Mandarin ability, I found a job as the Teacher's Assistant in the Mandarin Department. Despite not needing to take a foreign language, I decided to learn Japanese anyway. I had a US government scholarship that paid most of my tuition because Japanese (also French and Mandarin) were considered 'strategic' languages, and the government sensibly thought it important to have a pool of citizens who could speak the languages of potential conflict zones.

I suppose Japanese was still included because the memories of the Second World War fought against Japan had not yet faded from the government's memory. Other 'strategic' languages of that Cold War era included Arabic, Spanish, Russian, etc.

Curiously, despite my years focusing on the cultures of and living in Asia, most of my friends were Latinos, with one of my best friends (to this day) a Cubano whose family fled to Guatemala after Castro's revolution. It was a wonderful insight into a world I had neglected.

They taught me how to dance their various dances and, most importantly, the sideways swaying movement of the hips. Decades later, while living in southern California with my then Irish girlfriend, we learned salsa dancing. I remembered the proper swaying from side to side, whereas she, being Irish, was always hopping straight up and down like in their famous river dance.

Over the long Labor Day weekend I traveled with my Cubano friend to Guaymas, Mexico on the Sea of Cortez (the Gulf of California) on the Mexican mainland opposite to the peninsula of Baja California, not to be confused with Alta California in the US. We rented a car and traveled with two Latina classmates. I had a wonderful time discovering the incredible Mexican cuisine (NOT Tex-Mex!) and their Bohemia beer.

We bought two cases of Bohemia beer to bring back to the US. Being well traveled and well acquainted with US import restrictions, I knew we were well under the limits for four adults. The US Customs border agent asked to open our trunk. She noticed the beer and made an issue of it. I reminded her that we were within the legal limits. I was surprised when she told me that, according to Arizona State law, it was forbidden to bring into the state any alcohol from anywhere, not even from neighboring states like California.

She offered two suggestions. We could dump it into a dumpster that she pointed to, or we could drink it, but then she could not allow us to continue driving. I replied that we had a third option. José and I carried the cases of beer back into Nogales through the open gate in the chain link fence that divided the border. It reminded me of the towns in the old Western movies, of saloons with their small, swinging wooden doors and wooden plank sidewalks. There was a group of Mexican men standing on the corner with their cowboy hats and mustaches. We gave them our beer, which they very happily accepted. We walked back to the car and continued driving through the desert to Pheonix.

Though I had already met the requirement to speak a foreign language twice with Mandarin and French, I took the opportunity to learn yet another. I chose Japanese as it was by far the major economy of Asia at that time.

While studying my first semester of Japanese, I applied for and won a scholarship to study Japanese at the Institute of International Studies and Training (IIST) at the foot of Mount Fuji near Fujinomiya, about two hours south of Tokyo by car. It covered the room, two meals a day, tuition, books, etc. Half the student body was foreign students from various business schools around the world.

The other half was Japanese students. We shared business classes taught in English by various foreign business school professors. The Japanese had English classes. We had Japanese classes. The institute was part of Japan's Ministry of International Trade and Industry.

The dorms had four or six private rooms with a common bathroom with a Japanese soaking bath at one end of the corridor and a common living room at the entrance with sofas, chairs, and a table, covered with large manga graphic art novels and Japanese girlie magazines.

The girlie magazines were always full of nicely formed women in their twenties pretending to be girls in their mid-teens by (barely) wearing the official high school girl uniforms with their short skirts. I do not believe they were really high school girls due to laws protecting minors, but I am not sure. This fits in with the typical Asian males' predilection for teenage girls.

We ate together in the cafeteria twice a day. We visited the local grocery store once a week, where we bought what we could for dinners, the only meal we were responsible for ourselves. I usually made instant soup noodles in my room for dinner with lettuce and an egg. Because Japan has a 100 Volt system, my electric clock from the US, running on a 110 Volt system, ran about ten percent slower. My electric soup pot cooked slower, too.

I could see Mount Fuji from my window. One night we had an earthquake that shoved my bed with me asleep in it across the room, as a strong man could have done. The school was set in a forest in the foothills of the famous mountain. It was very rural, with dairy farms scattered along the lonely road uphill. For my exercise, I ran up the Fuji foothills to a war cemetery as my destination and back down to IIST. We organized and taught the Japanese students how to play a hash house harriers event. I managed to catch the hare.

Down the hill at a crossroads was a Japanese restaurant where I had horse sashimi.

The other foreigner in my dormitory was an American from the US, too. When he learned I practiced my martial arts in a small, windowless room with a large punching bag, he asked me if I would be his master. I told him I would not be his master, but he could train with me. But he was looking for a master to guide him in life.

Once, we caught a ride with a Japanese student to go somewhere south for the weekend. When we stopped at a rest stop on the highway to refuel, he disappeared. We had already driven about forty minutes. When I returned on Sunday, he was there. I have no idea how he returned. It would have been a long walk. Maybe the police took him back.

It was his first time away from home from whatever small town in the center of the US. He had a wife. After he tried to cut his wrists, they had to send him home. The director of the institute called me into his office. I had to explain everything I knew about him and the events leading up to his rash attempt at self-destruction. That all happened within the first month.

On most weekends, I caught rides with my fellow Japanese students to either Tokyo or points south. I often stayed with my Nepali friend in Tokyo. He had a typical tiny Tokyo apartment with a small kitchenette and a toilet in a room the size of a closet (had to go to the public baths to shower). We slept on futons on the tatami floor in the only other room, which also served as the dining, living, and sleeping area. Despite the very damp and cold winters, followed by extremely hot and humid summers, there was no heating or air conditioning.

Traditional floors in Japanese homes are tatami mats fitted tightly together. They are made of woven rush reeds with a rice straw center in a cloth frame. They have a standard size of three by six feet (90 by 180 cm). Landlords advertise their apartments for rent by how many tatami mats it has to indicate the size. The floor has a degree of softness that makes it pleasant to walk on without shoes. One always removes their shoes before entering a Japanese home. After fifty years of being a Japanese colony, Taiwan has the same style of floors and the habit of not wearing shoes in the house.

As is normal, there was no furniture in my Nepali friend's place, except a low table for eating where we could sit on the tatami floor and place our legs under the table in a space built into the floor below it. There also was a thick tablecloth that reached the floor, with a heater attached under the tabletop to keep our legs warm. We had to wear coats above our waists.

The public baths were not too far away. After washing ourselves in the shower, we soaked in the extremely hot soaking bath. We hurried back home through the ice and snow. The foreigners staying nearby would have a few cold beers on the way home and then wonder why they were catching awful colds. My advice is always to at least consider what the locals do in any given situation.

I learned how to handle the nearly boiling water in a Japanese bath. Once you manage to slowly enter the large, steaming bath, do not move. After a few minutes, the thin layer of water surrounding us reaches our body temperature. If you were to suddenly move, you would break that layer of relatively cooler water, and the steaming hot water reaches the body, requiring you to readjust again.

I did not make any friends with my fellow Japanese students because of the country's education system. There are two Japans. There is the elite who work either in government or the big companies, and then there is everyone else. The path to either destination is determined by national exams at various grades in both the primary and secondary school systems. If the students pass an exam, then they continue on the path to the better schools, followed by more exams continuing to the entrance exams to the best universities.

If a student fails any of the exams, then he or she is placed into the lesser schools. The elite students enter the best universities. At this point, they have succeeded in finding a respectable position in society. All that remains during the university years is passing a job interview with the most prestigious company or government ministry in the few months before graduation.

Everyone else continues on their path of lesser education to a lower-level university or trade school. These people make up most of society, from truck drivers to schoolteachers. Since they lack a reason to be arrogant, they are much friendlier and 'real'.

Mt. Fuji Outside My Window

Japan 1988

How I Cured the National Hubris

The year was 1988, and Japan was on the rise. Large Japanese commercial empires had bought the Pebble Beach golf course in California for 950 million US dollars, the Rockefeller Center in New York for 1.4 billion US dollars, and spent the most on any work of art in history at auction in 1987 for about 40 million US dollars for a vase of sunflowers by Van Gogh. Claims were made that the Imperial Palace in the center of Tokyo was worth more than the entire US stock market. Books explained how the US was on a permanent decline due to it being multiracial and multicultural. Japan would soon replace the US as the world's economic superpower. It was the Japan who could say 'no'.

My elite Japanese classmates were often insufferable. One day I received an opportunity to put a stop to this trajectory of becoming the world's economic hegemon. I received a chain letter in the mail. Unfortunately, they were fairly common in the days before the internet. A chain letter, coming from someone anonymous with no return address, always had the same message. The recipient had to forward the same letter to twenty or thirty other people within thirty days, or dire consequences would follow.

Normally, I threw such letters away without a second thought. I figured that whatever disaster would befall me would be so small to such a minor player in the world as me, I would probably not even notice it. In the grand scale of disasters, it would only be a low-lying speed bump. Certainly, I would never send it on to anyone I knew. I often wondered if the Post Office did not send these letters to increase stamp sales.

But this time, I was inspired. I went to the institute's library and looked up the thirty largest Japanese corporations with their CEO's and company addresses. Then I sent that chain letter to each of them. I imagine his secretary opened the letter, shook her head, and simply threw it out without wasting his time. The thirty days came and went, and Japan soon after entered the worst recession from which it has not fully recovered to this day. Vengeance is mine, sayeth the Lord!

On my first weekend trip, I traveled south by train to Nagoya. I checked in at the large, modern, and clean youth hostel. I was the only one staying there. It was freezing cold as I wandered around town. There was not much interesting to see. Being a great fan of traditional Chinese teahouses in Taiwan, I tried to find a Japanese equivalent.

I could find nothing that fits the description of 'traditional'. However, I did find a modern café. I asked the girl working there in my still primitive Japanese where I could find such a tea house. I understood from her reply that I should talk to the café owner, who would return in about an hour. So, I wandered the frigid streets until then.

When I returned, the friendly owner was already there. He spoke little English. Nonetheless, he took me to exactly what I had in mind. We sat at a low table and had traditional Japanese tea, which differs greatly from the Chinese version. One may remember my description of traditional Chinese tea in the Taiwan chapters.

Instead of a central teapot of tea that is poured into small cups as is the Chinese custom, the Japanese version is that each person has a large, nicely glazed ceramic bowl. Green tea is most common in Japan and is finely cut, almost to powder. This is placed in one's bowl, and boiling water is poured over it. Then, with a bamboo whisk, one briskly mixes the tea and hot water together. Finally, with both hands, one lifts the bowl and drinks from it. The ambiance is wonderful, with traditional Japanese minimalist furniture and classical Japanese music playing in the background.

Afterwards, he took me to a traditional tavern called an akachochin (赤提灯), meaning 'red hanging lantern', referring to the two large paper red lanterns hanging outside beside the entrance. They are my favorite places in Japan. Later, I would seek them out and spend hours for dinner. They serve a wide variety of food on beautiful, small ceramic plates. One could order ten different dishes and wash them all down with saki and call it a wonderful meal.

The small, square, wooden tables are placed close together. Every time I went to one, I could only order maybe two dishes and one sake before a group of locals at a nearby table would call me over to join them. They also have the same sentiment as other parts of Asia that no one should ever drink alone.

I have had many excellent experiences practicing Japanese with a wide range of men at these taverns, from truck drivers to factory workers to small shopkeepers. They were splendid examples of the non-elite. The elite would rarely eat in such places. I say 'men' because I never saw a woman in any of them.

The akachochin I visited that day was owned by a friend of his who had hitchhiked around Canada for a year. He spoke English well. The three of us had a great time eating the wonderful food and drinking plenty of sake. Time passed quickly. It was already getting close to 2200, the curfew for the youth hostel. My new friend called the hostel and told them I was in good hands and not to worry about me. They would bring me there the next day.

It must have been after midnight when it was closing time. My newfound friend left for home. The tavern owner invited me to stay with him and his family, who lived upstairs. His wife prepared another delicious meal. With more sake, we watched the video of the movie Top Gun.

A few weeks later, my tea house friend invited me to stay with his family for the weekend of the Cherry Blossom Festival. Though still very cold, everyone gathers for competitions like three-legged and sack races with picnics under the beautiful pink blossoms. It is a wonderful tradition.

It turned out that both he and his wife were public school teachers. He owned the café as a side project. We had a fine dinner at his home with his wife and two young children. He gave me my Japanese name based on the characters of my Chinese name. The characters are the same (慕容天), but the pronunciation is different. In Mandarin, it is pronounced Murong Tian. In Japanese, it is Boyo Ten.

They honored me greatly by letting me be the first to use the hot tub before dinner. This honor is usually reserved for the man of the family, and then everyone else goes later without changing the hot water. As the guest of honor, they let the hairy foreigner use it first. Of course, one takes a full shower before getting into the hot tub. So, we are clean when we get in, but an occasional pubic hair may escape and float about. I kept up correspondence with him for many years until I lost his address.

Back at the institute, I remember walking through the classroom wing after classes. I heard sobbing coming from one of the rooms. I entered and found a Japanese girl student sitting in a chair surrounded by five big mid-Western boys from the US berating her. It looked like a struggle session during China's Cultural Revolution. Rather than Marxist socialist revolutionary cadres, they were evangelicals, even worse. I stopped their abuse, allowing her to escape in tears. They were too shocked by the devilish intervention to stop her from fleeing.

Shizuoka Province is where the institute is located. It reaches from Mt. Fuji to the coast. On the coastal flatlands, there are wasabi plantations. Wasabi is a type of horseradish and, so, is the root of a bush. Most people are familiar with wasabi from the spicy green paste that one mixes with soy sauce at Japanese restaurants. By the way, Japanese do not do that. They put a small bit of wasabi on the sushi or sashimi and eat it that way.

In Japan, they make various things from wasabi, including salty chips. I once stayed at a modern Japanese hotel and had the dinner buffet. For dessert, I went to the ice cream bar and gave myself a big bowl of green tea ice cream, one of my favorite flavors. My first bite told me it was, in fact, wasabi ice cream, as spicy hot as could be. They are the same green color. In Taiwan, they have pork flavored ice cream. Whatever floats the boat.

Among many things that I have only seen in Japan, one thing stands out more than the others. One night, I was walking through the small town of Fujinomiya when I passed a vending machine on the side of the street. There was nothing unusual about that until I noticed what was being sold. Besides large bottles of beer and saki, anyone could buy a liter of Japanese whisky at any hour of the day or night. There was no attempt to limit by age. Something like that could not exist in the US. The US government has even taken away all the cigarette vending machines that existed everywhere in my younger days.

During one of my weekend trips around Japan, I met a friendly young Japanese man of my age. We spent some pleasant time together. As was the polite custom then, we exchanged addresses. In my case, it was my mother's address. Months later, my mother received his letter, written in his schoolboy English, informing her he had met her son, whom he liked very much, and thought he was very gay. She knew me too well to know that the word he used was meant in the archaic sense of being jolly and easy-going.

There was a time when hitchhiking was common, even in the US. Nowhere was it as easy as it was in Japan. Sometimes cars stopped to give me a ride, even before I stuck my thumb out. The only time when it was nearly impossible was when it was raining. No one wanted my wet shoes touching the floor of their car. After all, this is a people who have different slippers for the home and for the bathroom. They have separate shoes for driving, changing their street shoes when entering and leaving their cars.

The only other country that came anywhere close to Japan was the UK. Before fear took hold, I hitchhiked in the US and picked up hitchhikers. Once in the countryside of North Carolina, I stopped and picked up a middle-aged man. He told me he wanted a ride to the next town, about twenty minutes away. It was on my way, and so I let him in. After a few minutes, he asked me how I knew he was not a psychopathic serial murderer.

Knowing it was a hypothetical question, I gave him a hypothetical answer. I replied that I was not worried. After all, what were the odds that two psychopathic serial killers would randomly ride in the same car together? He asked me to stop and let him out, as he suddenly remembered that his doctor had told him he should walk whenever he had the chance. I kindly let him out unmolested.

On another weekend trip, I met a group of factory workers at a big beer hall. They invited me to drink with them. They were all wearing women's shoes with plastic flowers (no high heels). I was staying at a ryokan, a traditional Japanese inn. They walked me back through the local streets, carousing and urinating like the Brussels boy statue along the way.

While I was in Japan, I applied for various professional jobs. A big construction equipment company wanted me to work for them. As we were finalizing the details, they asked me how large an apartment I needed, as they would provide one. I replied that I preferred something big enough for both me and my Taiwanese girlfriend. They called it off because they wanted me to marry a nice Japanese girl and become a company man. It was still the land of arranged marriages and company men. It is a man's world, even now. If I had worked with them, my life would have been very different and stranger. It is another example in life when I intuitively made the correct decision.

Many years later, while I was on a business trip there, I visited a supplier. I was in the president's office discussing something. There was a quiet rap at the bottom of his sliding traditional paper door. I thought a cat was scratching it. He called out, and a young woman slid the door open. She had a tray of tea for us, and she was on her knees!

On that same trip, we had a geisha entertain us at dinner with her shellacked hair, kimono, and painted white face. She entertained us with traditional Geisha dances, singing, and playing traditional music with a period stringed instrument. Another woman dressed normally as a non-geisha sat next to me and poured my drinks. She made it very clear that she was not a prostitute and was only making money for her university studies.

While it was still very much winter, a group of us, including mainly Japanese students, decided to climb Mount Fuji. I had winter boots, but nothing meant for climbing an icy mountain. Fortunately, I was given a climbing ice pick. It was just as well. At one point I fell and started sliding towards a sheer cliff, desperately trying to drive my pick into the ice. I finally did and stopped my fatal descent off the mountain.

Japan is a wonderful country. I love the people and greatly enjoyed my time there. I eventually did find a job with Siber Hegner, a Swiss company based in Zurich with a long history of over 150 years in Tokyo. They sent me to work in Hong Kong instead. I needed the work experience more than another language. So, my Japanese never reached the fluency threshold like my Mandarin did. In the end, Japan did not continue as the predominate economic power of the world, being well surpassed by China, no thanks to my fateful chain letter.

Climbing Mt. Fuji without Proper Boots and Already Slipping

1989

Bahrain, Greece, Turkey, Yugoslavia, Austria, Switzerland, And France

Bahrain 1989

The Persian Gulf

After a year working at Siber Hegner in Hong Kong, it was time for me to return to Thunderbird and finish my MBA. I took the long way home via Europe. My first stop was Bahrain in the Persian Gulf. The causeway that connects Bahrain to Saudi Arabia is twenty-five kilometers (fifteen miles) of bridges and islands.

This was my first trip to the Middle East and the Arab world. Bahrain is the most liberal of the Gulf States, but only in the relative sense of the word. Alcohol was available. So, at the beginning of every weekend, many Saudi men drive across the causeway for a weekend of booze and discrete womanly professionals. Even so, all women wore burkas in public.

The temperature was so hot (45 Celsius/114 Fahrenheit at the end of May) that I had to seek shelter out of the sun for much of the day. Open hours were from 0700 to 1300 and from 1700 to 1900 with a four-hour siesta in between. All the taxis were old, gas-guzzling US cars from the 1960's complete with powerful air conditioning, which, incredibly, the drivers never used.

I was dismayed when I passed a small local mosque. The men were inside worshiping their god, while the womenfolk waited in their black burkas on the steps outside, not even talking with each other like dogs waiting for their master outside a store or café. While taking a public bus, I saw a woman lift her burka up slightly to step on, revealing a very colorful robe above her ankle underneath. Burkas are like outdoor wear, which the women take off as soon as they return home.

The many construction sites were mostly being built by large Korean construction companies that brought in Koreans to do the work. The number of foreigners working in the Gulf States is astounding, from Filipina servants to Indian manual labor to English accents in the high-rise offices of international finance companies.

There are several places worth seeing in and around Manama, the capital. My three-day visa was enough time to walk away with an understanding of the small country. I filled these days with various interesting things to do and see. As is my custom, one of those things was to take a dip in every large body of water that was new to me. In this case, it was the Persian Gulf.

The Onion Man and Me

Greece 1989

Islands in a Wine Dark Sea

From Bahrain, my girlfriend and I flew to Athens. We visited all the necessary sites and museums. The ruins of the Acropolis and the incredible archeology museum were very impressive. I was surprised at how old and rundown the city was, with few modern office buildings and confusion everywhere. The central park was full of hungry feral cats, the poor dears.

It was very amusing to watch the changing of the guard in front of the capitol building with the guards in short skirts and pompoms, high stepping with their silly clown shoes across the entrance. They surely bring a smile and a chuckle to any tourist watching them. Compared to the Buckingham Palace guards in London, the only silly thing about them is their too-large hats made from Canadian bear fur. I doubt many tourists realize that it takes one black bear skin to make one hat.

After enough of that, I took the metro to Piraeus, the port for Athens. From there, I started my journey through the Aegean by ferry. The first stop was Mykonos, famous for its beach and nightlife, where the loud discos carry on well past dawn. I had no interest in this. Many islands support ten times more tourists than the native Greek population.

This is one reason Greeks generally do not like tourists. Thanks to its orthodox religion, Greece is a very conservative country. Old women in black will cause great grief to a young woman tourist who tries to enter a church with her bare shoulders, as if their god cares about the bare shoulders that he made himself for young women, according to their biblical myths.

Northern Europeans happily took to nude sunbathing, which also caused the old women great stress. Greece has come a long way far from its ancient, easy-going roots of Socrates and the nude Olympics, well lubricated with olive oil. In any case, they already let in the Trojan Horse of tourism with all the easy wealth it brings.

As is common at ferry ports, foreign passengers are met with a horde of touts offering places to stay. It is impossible to make an educated choice without a smartphone handy. One could only trust the photos the tout showed and determine if the price was reasonable. Luckily, the islands are small enough that, at worst, one might stay a twenty-minute walk from the town center or the beach.

Delos is a tiny island covered in UNESCO recognized ancient ruins. The ferry stopped here for a few hours. It is the birthplace of brave Apollo, the sun god, and beautiful Artemis, the moon goddess. It served as a neutral place amid the conflicts of the classical Greek city states.

In 30 BC, there were 30,000 people from across the Mediterranean and the Black Sea living there. No one lives there now. I remember it as a very peaceful place. I particularly enjoyed the mosaics of Dionysus riding a tiger and another where he rides a panther. As the god of wine and good times, I lament his expulsion by the Holy Orthodox Fathers. Perhaps it would be more accurate to say that he has been repressed, but not gone completely, if Kazantzakis and his friend Zorba, or Dassin's movie, Never on Sunday, are to be believed.

I continued by ferry to Paros and then to Santorini. Trips between the islands only take a few hours across the blue waters of the Aegean, passing by many small uninhabited islands, some mere rocks jutting up from the watery depths. The only other place that reminded me of these wonderful watery journeys was the Philippines.

The island towns shared the similar beautiful aesthetics of bright whitewashed walls with luscious blue roofs, window and door frames. Santorini is probably the cover girl of these very special islands. I visited the archeological ruins of an advanced civilization for its time (Minoan?) that was destroyed by a great volcanic eruption and earthquake in 1500 BC, which split the island in two and caused a very destructive tsunami affecting much of the Eastern Mediterranean.

By reading Plato's description from over a thousand years after the fact, many think this was the original site of Atlantis without the modern fairy tales surrounding it. Perhaps it was an allegorical fairy tale invented by Plato?

The next trip was on an overnight ferry to Heraklion, Crete. Heraklion is both the largest city and the capital. It is the location of the ancient Minoan city of Knossos, where Theseus killed the Minotaur in the labyrinth below. The half bull half man Minotaur was the son of the Minoan King and his lascivious Queen. How that came about involves the famous inventor Daedalus (Icarus was his son, who flew too close to the sun) and your Google search.

Large caravans of tourist buses overwhelmed Knossos. I wanted to escape them and visit the untouristed southern coast. It proved too difficult, as the public buses mainly ran along the northern coast. After some days there, it was time to continue to Rhodos (Rhodes). To get there required taking a ferry from Sitia on the far northeastern tip of Crete.

After arriving by early afternoon, an elderly man was at the bus station trying to interest travelers in staying at his guesthouse. I took him up on his reasonable offer. There his wife met us with the traditional hospitality of a plate of sweets and fruit with a glass of ouzo, a strong (around 50% alcohol) dry anise-flavored apéritif. It is remarkably similar to pastis (France), raki (Turkey), arak (Middle East), etc. in taste.

It was normal for hotels to keep one's passport until checkout. I suppose it was to prevent anyone from leaving without paying. Shortly after checking in to our Sitia guesthouse, my girlfriend told me she had forgotten her passport at the hotel we had stayed at the night before in Heraklion.

Being the chivalrous, generous-hearted man that I still am, I told her, no problem. I would go back and get it. No quarrels were necessary. So, back on the bus I went and returned to the hotel. They gave me her passport, remembering that we were traveling together. I took the next bus back, but it only stopped halfway. It arrived at the last stop five minutes after the last bus to Sitia had left.

It was 2000. I was stuck at a crossroads fifty kilometers (thirty miles) from Sitia. What to do? I stuck out my thumb and hitchhiked. A German living in Crete picked me up but only took me eight kilometers closer. I still had forty-two kilometers (twenty-six miles) to go. The darkness of night had already fallen. Walking along the lonely coastal road through forests, with the moon occasionally peaking down from its lofty perch, I tried to hitchhike the rest of the way. Every time a rare car came by, they veered far from me and sped away with tires screeching.

I asked myself, what was the worst thing that could happen? It was a fine night for a hike. If I walked fast, as was my custom then, it would only take me about eight or nine hours to return, enough time to catch the 0700 ferry to Rhodos. I could sleep on the ferry.

As I walked, I could hear an occasional helicopter flying above the trees. I was surprised by the panicking drivers' reaction to me. Finally, a car stopped. It was a taxi. He offered to take me to Sitia. I refused his offer as I was used to taxis charging exorbitant prices in times of need.

He told me to not be crazy and get in, offering to drive me there without charge, as he was going there anyway. He explained an even more important reason to get in. There was a prison escape on the island by a dozen foreign prisoners, who killed a few guards in the process. The police were looking for these foreigners and would shoot on sight. There I was, a foreigner walking on a remote road towards a ferry port to escape the island. The helicopters above were the police, who could not see me under the canopy of the trees. In the event, I returned by midnight with enough time to get some decent sleep.

The ferry to Rhodos took all day, passing various islands on the way. Rhodos is a medieval fortress that was once owned by the Templar Knights (a religious order of fighting monks), who were a constant thorn in the side of the Ottoman Empire a short distance away in Turkey. The Turks besieged the city several times. Their stone cannonballs scattered outside the city walls attest to that. The walls held until one day they did not.

Of course, there were hordes of tourists, but the city managed to absorb them relatively well. I visited much of the island, too. It was an Italian possession until the end of the Second World War. Mussolini rebuilt the Templar Palace of the Grand Master. That and the archeological museum in the basement with the ancient mosaics made it an interesting visit. I concluded my travels in Greece by taking the two-and-a-half-hour ferry to Marmaris on the Turkish coast facing Rhodos, arriving early evening. Thus, I completed my fascinating journey through the birthplace of much of Western civilization.

The Aegean through the City Gate

Turkey 1989

Ancient Crossroads

We arrived in Marmaris on the southwest coast of Turkey by ferry from Rhodos. Because the Turkish embassy in Greece only gave my Taiwanese girlfriend a short-term visa to visit, I asked the immigration officers at the ferry terminal if they could extend it for her. They suggested it would be easier to simply overstay the visa and pay the 88000 Lira fine. The exchange rate at the time was 2000 Lira to one US dollar, making the fine worth about forty-four US dollars. They knew their country well.

The exchange rate changed in our favor daily. Many times, throughout our six-week visit, if I delayed exchanging my US dollars by one day, the difference in lira would allow us to eat for free that day.

Marmaris was a small town that had become a very touristy resort destination. The costly yachts filling the marina attested to that fact. They certainly were not local fishing boats. I was glad to escape to Bodrum, a three and a half hour bus ride away.

Bodrum was only three quarters overrun with tourists. It is famous for being the site of the Mausoleum at Halicarnassus, one of the seven wonders of the ancient world. It was built in the fourth century BC. When I was there, it was just a large hole in the ground. I had been to another no longer existing wonder when I visited Rhodos, where its famous bronze Colossus stood 33 meters (110 feet) above the harbor. Built in the third century BC, it had long tumbled into the sea by an earthquake. The only ancient wonder that still stands today is the Pyramids of Egypt.

We visited Izmir, a major port and NATO naval base. Though there are few things to see there, we were finally away from the mobs of tourists. It felt great, and I realized that I preferred Turkey to Greece, even after removing the tourists from the equation.

This is mainly because Greece is religiously and socially very conservative and, at heart, the Greeks do not really like the tourists that have brought prosperity to many parts of the country. Like the Trojans of myth, it was the Greeks themselves who opened their country to the Trojan Horse of tourism. Though Turkey is a Muslim country, it is much more relaxed than Greece. The people are far friendlier and hospitable.

Continuing south by bus for one and a half hours, we arrived at the coastal resort town of Kusadasi, full of discos and tourists. The next day we went to visit Soke by a dolmus, a local minibus, which means 'stuffed' in Turkish, a very apt name for the very stuffed vehicles. Soke is the jumping off point for seeing three famous ruins.

The first was Priene. It was the site of various ruined temples laying in rubble, if visible at all. The most important one was the Temple of Athena. All that remains are five columns that were re-erected in 1965 (three meters/ten feet shorter than the originals). It was not impressive.

Considering the very irregular dolmus schedule, we decided to walk to the next ruined site, attempting to hitchhike along the way. Sure enough, a Turkish man picked us up soon after and took us to our next destination of Miletus at the mouth of the Meander River, the origin of the word 'meander'.

The ancient Greek theater is the most important thing there, but the whole ruined city was worth many hours. One may surmise that there was a lot of ancient Greek influence on the Turkish coast of the Aegean. That is because Greek city states dominated this coast, starting from over 4000 years ago. Miletus was the home of several famous Greek philosophers, including Thales (626 to 548 BC), who is considered the first real philosopher of Greece. It also created sixty colonies, mainly in the Black Sea region.

Afterwards, he took us to Didyma, the site of the incredible temple to Apollo. Thanks to our kind driver, we could condense a long day into half a day. We had lunch there, and I forced him to accept being my guest. He wanted to continue taking us to other places in the afternoon, but I was embarrassed by his generosity and had to decline. When he picked us up, he was on his way to some place else, though I never knew where.

He spoke no English. I, however, could speak about fifty Turkish words by then, enabling me to ask maybe fifteen questions or make fifteen statements. I always try to learn as much of the language of the different peoples I visit. Always. It is my way of showing respect to them. Nonetheless, our conversation was limited, to say the least. But he greatly appreciated my attempts.

It took us the rest of the afternoon to return to our guesthouse in Kusadasi by several dolmuses. The next day we took another dolmus to Selcuk. From there, the wonderful Ephesus is a three-kilometer walk (about two miles) on a mulberry tree canopied country lane. It is as impressive as I was led to believe. So were the tourist crowds. In a small archeological museum nearby, we saw the famous ancient fat fertility goddess with many breasts. Man's fascination with women's breasts has never changed. Good news for the continuation of the species!

After visiting Ephesus, we took the five-hour bus trip to Pamukkale. This town in the country's interior is famous for its multiple levels of cotton white terraces made from the flowing of the mineral-rich thermal waters down the hillside. What I enjoyed most was swimming in a winding lagoon among submerged Roman ruins. It was as touristed when we visited it as it was 2200 years before by Roman tourists.

We took another five-hour bus ride to Antalya, back on the Mediterranean coast. Besides yacht-filled marinas and expensive tourist restaurants, it is known for Hadrian's Gate, built to commemorate that great Roman emperor's visit in 130 AD. The next morning, we traveled seven hours by bus into the interior to Konya.

Konya is famous as a pilgrimage destination for Sufis. It is the location of the tomb of Jalaluddin Rumi, the founder of the Muslim Mevlana order. They are best known for their whirling dervishes. I saw this fascinating method of meditating and praying through dance. It is incredible to watch. To me, the founder was even more fascinating.

Jalaluddin Rumi is better known as simply Rumi in the West. He was a poet born in Afghanistan in 1207 and died in Konya in 1273. He was a Muslim mystic, writing mainly in Persian. Wine, women, and song were common subjects in his poetry. Regarding the myriad religions of the world, he also wrote that though the lamps are different, they all produce the same light. What a refreshing change from what much of the world sees Islam today!

Ankara, the capital of the country, was a mere three hours by bus. There, we visited the delightful ethnographic museum with its wonderful collection of richly carved wooden doors and beautiful old books from a different time. The Anatolian Civilizations Museum was fascinating, introducing the long-gone empires of the Hittites, Haris, Phrygians, Urartus, etc. I learned a lot about carpets at the bazaar. Turkish and Persian carpets are some of my favorite things. I eventually bought two large ones in Istanbul and shipped them to the US.

We visited the tomb of Ataturk, the founder of modern Turkey. He was a member of the Young Turks, a reformist group trying to modernize the Ottoman Empire before the First World War. He was a successful general who fought in the many wars at the beginning of the twentieth century during the dismantling of the empire in the face of numerous nationalist movements in the Balkans and a war with Italy over control of Libya.

The decrepit Ottoman Empire joined Germany and the Central Powers in the First World War. Ataturk came to prominence as leader of Turkish forces that defeated the Allied invasion of Gallipoli, a defeat that caused Winston Churchill, the Minister of the British Admiralty, to resign in disgrace. He later resurfaced as Prime Minister and led Britain to victory in the Second World War.

After the Ottoman surrender in 1918, there were another five years of war against the Armenians, Greeks, and the old regime of the Allied-supported Ottoman Empire. He vanquished all enemies and, in 1923, proclaimed the Republic of Turkey. He served as the first president of modern Turkey until he died in 1938.

As president, he successfully modernized and industrialized his country, transforming it from being the 'sick old man of Europe' to the vibrant country we know today. One of his most important modernizations was to raise women to be equals in society. He severely restricted Islam's influence, creating the first secular Muslim country. He forbade women from wearing hijabs in any public building. I do not remember seeing any woman in a hijab when I was there. In short, he deserves to be called the 'Father' of his country.

Next, we traveled by bus to Ürgüp in the Cappadocia region. This area is famous for its odd rock formations and ancient towns built underground in extensive networks of caves. People still live in some of them. Legend has it that the local people built these underground towns to protect themselves against marauding raiders about a thousand years ago.

A Dutchman and the two of us shared a taxi tour for 15000 lira (7.50 US dollars) that took us to all the major sights in the region. The trip lasted about nine hours. The tour included the towns of Güzelyurt, Ürgüp, and Göreme. Besides the underground towns, we visited cave churches from the early Byzantine era, a famous pottery village, and many other things besides. It was the end of June, and the sun was strong. I wore a bandana the whole time. Despite this, I had a slight sunstroke and had to spend the following few days in the cool of my bed until I recovered.

Our next destination was Kayseri, known to the early Christians as Caesarea. The bus took nine and a half hours. The following morning, we continued to Amasya, approaching the Black Sea region, requiring another bus trip of seven and a half hours. This was the center of the once powerful Pontic kingdom. The tombs of the kings were carved into the cliffs facing the Yesil River and dominating the town from above.

The Kingdom of Pontus lasted from 281 to 63 BC. It was led by four kings named Mithridates. The fourth one (Mithridates IV) waged an initially successful war against Rome, conquering all of Roman Asia. Eventually Rome conquered the Ponts in 63 BC, ending that chapter of history.

We continued to the city of Sivas, four hours away. Sivas has many beautiful Muslim sites, including an impressive mosque. Continuing our journey through central Anatolia, we arrived at the mainly Kurdish city of Kahta. This is the jumping off point to visit the incredible Mount Nemrut.

Staying mainly in lower cost guesthouses, we often slept on the large flat roofs where it was much cooler with the night breeze. Kahta was no different, though I remember not sleeping well because of the too strong wind. I slept little that night anyway, as we had to get up at 0130 to catch the tour to see the sunrise from the mighty Mount, two hours away.

Once we arrived, about fifty other tourists walked with us up the stony path to the top. We had to wait another forty-five minutes for the sun to rise. The crowd and the chilly wind sent us to the western side of the peak, where no one else was and the wind was somewhat blocked. Obviously, I did not go through all this just to see the sun rise from a remote mountaintop, the tallest of the eastern end of the Taurus Mountains (2100 meters/7000 feet).

This is the strange site of a tomb sanctuary with a curious group of statues built at the behest of King Antiochus (ruled from 70 to 31 BC) of the kingdom of Commagene. This minor kingdom served as a buffer state between Rome, Armenia, and Persia. It maintained its independence from 163 BC to 17 AD, when Rome finally made it a province. Because of its geographic location, it was heavily influenced by Persian, Roman, Armenian, and Greek cultures.

Considering how minor this kingdom was, this stone complex atop Mount Nemrut must count as one of the greatest tributes to the hubris of man in that very crowded arena. As was common in ancient times, kings usually started building their huge, complex tombs shortly after ascending the throne. In this case, he started construction in 69 BC and completed it in 34 BC. He could enjoy his tomb for the three years before his death.

The statues are of him sitting in the middle surrounded by two eagles, two lions, and various gods who were composites of Greek and Persian deities such as Herakles/Artagnes (better known as Hercules), Zeus/Oromasdes, Apollo/Mithras, etc. What makes this so laughable is that this relatively minor character considered himself the equal of the gods. A stone carving shows him shaking hands with Herakles/Artagnes. The statues were about three meters/ten feet tall. The heads have all since toppled onto the ground below. Luckily for us, he thoughtfully had their names inscribed on their various stone thrones.

While everyone else waited for the sun, we had the main site all to ourselves. When everyone arrived on the western side after the sun rose, we proceeded to the eastern side. It worked out well that way. On the bus ride back, we crossed a river on a still functioning Roman stone bridge. We arrived back by 0900.

Swimming among Roman Ruins

Turkey 1989

The Fertile Crescent

With a full day ahead of me and the energy of a young man in his twenties, we continued to Urfa, a three-hour bus ride away. It was called Edessa before Islam came. We passed over the Euphrates River and arrived at the upper end of the Fertile Crescent, the birthplace of occidental civilization. Nearby is the oldest temple in the world at the Neolithic site of Göbekli Tepe, built around 9000 BC. This was before pottery and agriculture. The people who built this extensive temple complex were still hunter-gatherers. However, the birth of agriculture occurred soon after.

The city claims to be the birthplace of Abraham, causing it to be the gathering point for the most conservative Turkish Muslims. Most historians agree he was born in the Sumerian city of Ur, far to the south in present day southern Iraq. This is how I was taught in high school. In religion, faith is more important than facts.

I am always fascinated by how people can be so violently emotional about things that are highly doubtful to discerning minds. I remember decades later when I visited the Tomb of the Holy Sepulchre in Jerusalem. One could get in line that went out to the street and beyond to see the tomb of Jesus, or one could bypass all that and enter to just visit the interior of the church. I chose the latter. As I walked past the gaping pilgrims in front of the empty hole in the ground, I remarked, “Thank the Lord, at least it’s empty!” They groaned in agreement, while my irony completely escaped them.

Diyarbakir was our next destination, a three-hour crammed dolmus ride away. The most famous site is the city fortress on the banks of the Tigris River, the other river bounding the Fertile Crescent on the east. It is the largest Kurdish majority city in Turkey.

The most memorable thing for me was the bizarre horde of children that fell upon me and their odd reactions. Some threw stones at me while others held my hands. Some grabbed my a-hole while others laughed and waved at me. Others threw water and watermelon rinds at me. Finally, a ten-year-old boy led me away from that crazy encounter. He spoke quite good English and was well acquainted with the USA.

We took a bus for seven hours to Van in eastern Turkey. It sits by the lake of the same name. We visited the ancient (800 BC) Van Fort, situated high on a hill. From there we could see the shimmering lake in the late afternoon sun on one side and on the other the strange sight of the building foundations of the old Armenian city still visible as outlines from beneath the grass-covered ground. Before the butchery of the events during and after the First World War against the Armenians, it was a major city of those people. Now it is mainly Kurdish.

Walking back, we met two young sisters of about nine and ten years old, struggling with large containers of water that they had filled at a well. They had quite a walk ahead of them. So, I carried the heavy containers for them. I made another two little friends.

The next day, we took a boat out to an island where the old Armenian Church of the Holy Trinity sat. Armenians built it in 917. The carvings on the walls of the exterior were in fine shape, unlike the frescos inside. Armenia was the first officially Christian country, having converted in 301. Neighboring Georgia followed soon after.

We left Van early morning and arrived in Doğubeyazıt five hours later. This Kurdish town is a border crossing into Iran. It was the capital of the Kurdish Republic of Ararat from 1927 to 1931. From the ruined palace on the border one can see the republic's namesake, Mount Ararat, the supposed site of the biblical fable of Noah's ark. The snow-covered mount lies in Armenia, fifteen kilometers/ten miles to the northeast.

After another five-hour bus ride, we arrived in Erzurum to the north. Since the average altitude of eastern Anatolia, the parts we traveled through, was about 2000 meters/6500 feet, the temperature was very pleasant for July. A university girl showed us around the city, practicing her English.

The next evening, we took the overnight bus to Trabzon on the Black Sea coast. Most of the sites to see were historic Greek churches that had been turned into mosques. We visited the abandoned thousand-year-old Sumela Monastery an hour and a half outside the city. It was mostly in ruins, but the location in a pine forest high up on a cliff face made the trip quite pleasant.

I sought out and found a small flat space by the Black Sea. It would be a major stretch of the truth to call it a beach. Nonetheless, it allowed me to wade into that dark sea. Following my custom, I could add another major body of water to my growing list.

As every high school student should know, Constantinople fell to Mehmed II, the Ottoman conqueror, in 1453, thus ending the Byzantine Empire. But did it? In fact, no, it did not. Trabzon continued as a rump state until it, too, fell to Mehmed II in 1461. However, there were in fact two other Byzantine rump states that survived even later, including Theodoro in the Crimea and Epirus in western Greece. Both succumbed in the years 1475 and 1479, respectively, twenty-six years after the fall of Constantinople.

Many decades later, I was in a pub in Hong Kong, talking with a group of my peers from the UK. I mentioned the date 1453 and the fall of Constantinople (pertinent to the conversation). They were shocked into silence. They asked me how it was possible that someone from the US would know such a thing.

I replied that besides being an extremely important date in European history, not all Americans from the US are yahoos. Of course, when I added the part about Trabzon, Theodoro, and Epirus surviving another twenty-six years, something their high schools did not teach them, they were completely blown away. Mine did not teach me that part either. I learned that factoid on my own.

Six weeks had passed since we had started our journey in Turkey. It was time to visit Istanbul before continuing our adventures across Europe and returning to the US to complete my MBA at Thunderbird in Phoenix, Arizona. The fall semester, starting in September, was fast approaching. I compared our options. We could take an overnight boat, a plane, or an overnight bus. The bus was the more economical choice. Being still young and resilient, we could sleep badly but still function well the next day.

As I shared about the local man who drove us to see the sights, I experienced the most amazing generosity from the Turkish people. Very often we met young Turks who spoke English in the city streets. They often invited us home to have a wonderful meal with their parents. After years of travel, I learned how to read strangers by looking into their eyes to know if they are honest or not. They always were.

Turkish food is one of the great cuisines of the world. Their specialty is eggplant in all its guises. Another wonderful thing is the wood-burning ovens in many neighborhoods across the country that make wonderful Turkish pizzas called pide. It is well worth the wait in line for one to come right out of the oven and into your hands. They are good for one or two people. They are made in the shape of boats and come with such tasty toppings as minced meat, cured beef, cheese, etc.

There is a very peculiar thing that I experienced in Turkey and nowhere else. I was traveling with a Taiwanese girlfriend at the time. As we walked about very often, young Turkish men would call out to her with a few simple Japanese words, assuming she was from there. It infuriated her, being exceedingly anti-Japanese because of their invasion of China during the Second World War. But what blew their minds was when I, not her, answered them in Japanese.

My curiosity was too overwhelming, so I asked them how they knew any Japanese words in the first place. Dozens across Turkey all told me the same thing. They had Japanese girlfriends who taught them. They showed me photos of them together. Now, I was really curious. They had never traveled to Japan. How did they ever have the chance to meet Japanese women?

Later, I figured it out. As a grand generalization, young Japanese women go to Turkey to play with the men before returning to their straight and boring lives in Japan. Particular groups of people prefer certain countries for their pleasures. Gays like traveling to Thailand and Sri Lanka. Western women go to India to rent their boy toys for their holiday flings. Gay pedophiles go to the Philippines. Hetero pedophiles go to Cambodia. Etc.

The bus delivered us to Istanbul at 1000 the next morning. We stayed at a hotel in the area of Sultanahmet, where the Hagia (Sancta) Sophia, the Blue Mosque, and many of the famous tourist sites of this great historic city are found. With a list of all the magnificent sites in hand, we proceeded to systematically visit them. I will not list them all here, as a simple Google search can give an idea. Suffice it to say, Istanbul is one of the great cities of the world. I would not mind living there for a while.

This modern, secular city with a population of around sixteen million started as a Greek colony named Byzantium, founded in the seventh century BC. In 324 AD, Emperor Constantine I (the Great, emperor from 306 to 337) reunited the broken Roman Empire, rendered by civil wars. He chose this minor city to be his capital for the entire empire in 330 AD. He named it after himself: Constantinople.

It remained the capital of the Eastern Roman Empire until the Turks conquered it in 1453, renaming it Istanbul. It then became the capital of the Ottoman Empire until 1922, when the empire was abolished and Ataturk moved the capital to Ankara. I call it 'Eastern Roman' because, though we refer to it as the Byzantine Empire, it really was a continuation of the Roman Empire. The Byzantines certainly thought so, though the city of Rome itself was forever lost.

The city served as the ancient crossroads between Europe and the Middle East, and between the Black Sea and the Mediterranean. It sits squarely on the European side of the Bosporus. Most everything of the Byzantium culture, especially pertaining to the Greek Orthodox Church, has been Islamized. For example, the old churches are all mosques now.

I could wax poetically about the grand Topkapi Palace of the Ottomans, the wonderful Blue Mosque, the underground cisterns, the smells and colors of the Grand Bazaar, and many more besides. But I will just mention a place off the beaten track. It is the Adalar Islands (Prince Islands) in the Sea of Marmara. They can only be reached by ferry. The ferry trip itself is worth it, as one can view Istanbul from a different angle. These quiet residential islands are free of cars. Instead, there are horse-drawn carriages to get around. I just enjoyed wandering the tree-covered streets. If I ever lived in Istanbul, I would live there.

Something of note is the number of incredibly friendly street cats and dogs. They patiently allow you to pet them without snarling, hissing, or running away. If you are sitting on a park bench, do not be surprised if a street cat does not leap onto your lap. I have visited many cities in the world, and only in Istanbul are these small street urchins so friendly. They are so because they are cared for by the kind and humane Turkish people. Though they live on the streets, they are not homeless, as all homes are theirs. One can watch the Turkish documentary, Kedi, exactly on this subject.

I happened to be in Istanbul on the day of Eid al-Adha, a major holiday throughout the Muslim world. It is the Festival of Sacrifice. It celebrates the Prophet Abraham/Ibrahim's willingness to sacrifice his son, Isaac, following God's command. According to the tale, the obedient father takes his son to a mountaintop, binds him, and draws his knife to do the ugly deed. God stops him at the last minute, convinced that he chose the correct man to found a new monotheist religion and a kingdom for his chosen people.

This is a day that I call the 'slaughter of the innocents'. On every green patch of grass across the city, groups of men slit the throats of thousands of bleating lambs. To say I was shocked is an understatement, especially since I had no idea what it was about. I thought the city had suddenly and collectively gone insane.

I went to the post office to ship the two carpets I had bought back to the US by ocean freight. The freight cost one and a half times more than the carpets. As I returned from shipping it, I walked along a lonely street bordered on one side by the brick wall of a tall building.

There was a pair of Turkish men in front of me. One was bent down as if he had a stomachache, and his friend was helping him. They slowed until they stopped while I was fast approaching them. I quickly sensed that another two were approaching me from behind, closing the distance between them and me. When I felt a hand go for my pocket, I immediately sprang sideways out into the street like a loaded spring.

They did not expect that and scampered away. This was the only time in my life that someone tried to rob me while I was aware of it. I was pickpocketed before, during these early travels, once in China, once in India, and once in the Soviet Union. What really stuck with me was that all four of the would-be thieves were carrying Muslim prayer beads.

After all these adventures in Turkey for over six weeks, it was time to continue our journey to the West. The plan was to take a bus from Istanbul through Bulgaria, Yugoslavia, and Hungary. This was when the Soviet Union was still very much alive, but not at all well. Unknown to all the world at the time, the Berlin Wall would fall less than four months later (November 9, 1989).

We needed visas to visit these countries. The Bulgars and the Yugoslavs were quite easy about it. Hungary proved too difficult, and so our plan changed to exit Eastern Europe via Austria. The day came, and we left Turkey behind us.

The warm glow that those memories still give my heart today will always make Turkey one of my favorite countries. I returned twenty-five years later to Istanbul. Then, I saw the changes wrought by Erdogan and his attempts to move away from the secular country that Ataturk founded. That saddens me. Fortunately, the incredible memories of my first trip will always remain.

Newly Found Turkish Friend

Europe 1989

The French Foreign Legion, Anyone?

My choice of a bus company for the journey from Istanbul, Turkey to Salzburg, Austria, was a huge mistake. The trip proved to be an even more unpleasant experience than the four pious thieves who tried to rob me while counting their prayer beads. The bus had two drivers. My seat was right behind theirs.

When it was time to change drivers, they did something my eyes could not believe, though it happened right in front of me. As the bus was hurtling down the highway, they changed drivers without even slowing a bit. The relieving driver climbed into the driver's seat behind the one still driving. The other driver then exited the seat after the other driver took the wheel. It was something clowns would do in a circus, but without the mortal danger to all the passengers. They did it because they thought it was fun.

They stopped before the Bulgarian border to buy a huge load of disposable diapers to smuggle into Bulgaria. Basic consumer goods like this and toilet paper, tampons, toothpaste, etc. were always in short supply in socialist command economies where the plans never worked out. We passed through Bulgaria during the night, so I saw very little. Ten years later, I would return for a proper visit.

The bus was full of various Egyptians, Tunisians, Sikhs, etc. Half did not make it past the Bulgarian border. The other half did not make it past the Yugoslav border. I was curious to see a long stream of Turks leaving Bulgaria, crossing the border while pushing carts full of all their worldly belongings. I never learned what that was about.

It took all the next day to cross Yugoslavia from south to north. We paused at a few rest stops along the way. I saw one curious and unforgettable sight. It was a Yugo, famous for being one of the worst quality cars ever built. The worthless engine was taken out, and the car was being pulled by two horses with the family sitting inside.

We stopped in Beograd, the nation's capital. It was as dreary and gray as I had thought it would be. I returned over twenty years later after it became the capital of Serbia. We saw Zagreb in the distance, the current capital of Croatia, as we passed by on the highway. Suddenly, a young woman from the US cried out to stop the bus. She had bought her ticket to Zagreb, but the drivers were not stopping. Finally, tired of hearing her desperate cries, they stopped on the side of the highway and let her off. They drove off, leaving her standing there with her luggage beside her, the city of Zagreb in the far distance, and tears rolling down her face.

I felt sorry for her, but there was nothing I could do. Little did I know at the time that they would treat me far worse. Our tickets were to Salzburg. They did not stop there, but at the Austrian German border, over ten kilometers/six miles away. It was 0100 with no way to Salzburg except to walk.

Hitchhiking was out of the question at that hour. I approached a car parked by the side of the road near the border crossing to try to get a ride. When I walked up to the passenger's side to ask, the woman sitting there screamed, and the man driving the car screeched away as fast as he could. We walked for over three hours with our heavy backpacks, finally arriving at the Salzburg train station by 0400, very cold and tired. I knew it would be the only place open so early. I dozed for a few hours until the youth hostel opened. There we could sleep until 1400 when they tossed everyone out for the rest of the afternoon. They were more generous than most youth hostels, which toss everyone out at 0900 or 1000 in the morning. That was without a doubt the worst experience I had traveling until even now. That and the attempted mugging in Istanbul clouded my otherwise positive experience with the Turks.

Though I had visited Salzburg thoroughly six years before, I gave a quick tour of the highlights for my girlfriend. Soon after, we caught the train west to Innsbruck, the alpine capital of Tyrol Province. This is a beautiful city, even for non-skiers like me. In my mind, it rivals Salzburg, especially given the tasteless marketing of Mozart in his birthplace.

After only a day of visiting, we continued by train until the line ended at the foot of the Alps. From there, we took a bus across the border into Liechtenstein and on to the capital town of Vaduz. The entire population is less than 40,000. It is a semi-constitutional monarchy led by a prince, who does not rate being a king, according to the arcane rules of monarchy. It was most famous for printing postage stamps for many countries around the world. The country itself is not more than a postage stamp in size, only twenty-five kilometers/fourteen miles from north to south, making it 160 square kilometers/90 square miles in total.

I was surprised at how many tourists with their tour buses crowded the small town. It was fortunate for us that we fell in with a group of Taiwanese tourists who gave us a ride on their tour bus to Zurich, Switzerland. They loved me mainly because of my years living in their country and being able to speak their language of Mandarin. We had a lot in common.

After arriving, we walked around Zurich for the rest of the day. The next day I contacted Siber Hegner, the company I had worked for in Hong Kong just a few months before. They treated us very well, including a wonderful Swiss dinner and a trip up the nearby snow-covered Mount Titlis (3300 meters/10000 feet high) by cable car. It was the first time my Taiwanese girlfriend had seen snow. She played in it like a little child. That was worth the trip alone.

After Zurich, we took the train to Luzern, a beautiful city with wooden covered bridges and old murals on the walls. Due to the excellent national train system, we could visit several towns on the same day on the way to Montreux, stopping at Interlocken, Spiez, and Zweisimmen. Montreux is in the French-speaking part on Lake Geneva, where I went for a frigid swim.

The next day, we continued to Lausanne, which sits on the northern shore of Lake Geneva. From there, it was a short train ride to Geneva. We stayed at the university dormitory, basically the only place I could afford. It was available because of the summer break, as it was the end of July.

We had crossed Switzerland from east to west by train. I did not believe all the talk about how beautiful Switzerland is. I mean, how can a country be that beautiful? But indeed, it can be. Of course, I was there in the summer when every window box and yard was covered in a riot of amazing colors and varieties of flowers. With all the medieval castles, cathedrals, and town centers, one could lose oneself in another time.

Lyons in France was only a two-hour train trip away. We stayed at a homeless shelter near the train station since I was, in fact, homeless then. I cooked our dinner in the communal kitchen. The kitchen TV was showing a soft porn film with long 'love' scenes full of orgasmic sounds and excitement. It was just another reminder that Toto was not in Kansas anymore (a reference to The Wizard of Oz).

The next day, as we walked through the busy train station, I passed a French Foreign Legion recruitment office. Stopping in front for a moment, I seriously considered that possible path in a life of adventure as a quasi-official French mercenary. I give myself credit for walking away. I was leading a much more pleasant and interesting life of adventure already.

After passing through that bit of silly temptation, we went to the ticket window to buy our tickets to Paris. The ticket seller asked if we were a couple. I replied that we were, but I had nothing to prove that. She said that it was unnecessary, and we saved 50%. This is only one small proof that Paris is the city for lovers. We took the high-speed TGV train. Two hours later, we arrived at the Gare de Lyon in less than 40% of the normal travel time.

It was my third trip to Paris. Without cell/mobile phones, booking.com or the like, finding a place to stay was the first necessary thing to do before leaving the station. There was the usual tourist office helping visitors find a hotel that was in all the city train stations. But I decided to do things differently this time.

I bought a phone card, entered the nearest phone booth with my Let's Go Europe guidebook, a great tome used by those from North America, and I called each of the hotels recommended. They were all full. Considering it was the beginning of August and every tourist from the US or Canada was trying to book the same dozen or so hotels, it was not surprising.

Since I was traveling with a woman, two bunks in a youth hostel dormitory were more expensive than one room in a hotel, seedy as it might be. So, I returned to the tourist booking office. Based on my criteria, they called a hotel and made a reservation for me. When I arrived, it was the same one they had sent me on my previous two visits! With a little time, the next morning, I found a superior hotel in a better location for half the price. Incredibly, it also included a shower and toilet in the room.

The first order of business after settling in was to book our flight back to the US. I found a reasonably priced charter flight to Los

Angeles, from where I could buy a low-cost flight to Pheonix, Arizona, where my business school, Thunderbird, is located. I bought the tickets for a flight in two weeks.

With that done, I bought two weeklong passes to visit all the museums we could fit in that brief time for forty-eight francs. I must have missed something, because I noticed most tourists were buying day passes for fifty-two francs. With our metro passes, we were ready to see the City of Light. It never gets old.

Whenever I saw billboards with topless women advertising anything from shampoo to biscuits, I had to smile. Toto was enjoying his last few moments before he had to return to puritanical Kansas. We had dinner at a Corsican restaurant run by a Marxist Corsican separatist who sold the meals at cost. I enjoyed speaking French with everyone I met, even with Marxists.

The most amazing thing I saw there was the newly opened Musee d'Orsay, which was originally the Gare d'Orsay where the trains from the English ferry arrived, as I did on my first trip to Paris. It is my favorite museum in the world. They kept the original Beaux Artes iron frame and other Arte Nouveau elements of the original train station and made it into a museum of all things Impressionist, my favorite art style.

We visited a Frenchman at his home, whom we had met in Istanbul. He was unusual in that he converted to Islam. We spoke for hours about this. I asked him about the idea of having four wives and how that could fit with life in Paris in 1989. He explained that a man needs that many wives. Just think, for example, on any given night, one wife could be on her time of the month, another could be sick, and another might be angry over some petty thing. So, at least he would have one to service him. He did not, alas, have four wives, nor even one.

France had a service at the time that matched drivers with passengers who would share the cost of the trip. I found one such driver who was going to Luxembourg. Arriving by car gave me the chance to make a day trip of it. The small city did not impress me, which made me glad I had left all my things in the hotel in Paris. I traveled there alone because my Taiwanese girlfriend could not get a visa to visit. She was stuck in Paris, a wonderful place to be stuck.

I bought a bottle of cheap table wine from a food store for the train trip back. On the train, I met a French soldier, a native of Martinique on leave, though still in his uniform. I shared my wine with him. Passing the bottle back and forth made the return very enjoyable.

Being a charter flight, the charter company could not be sure when the plane would leave. Perhaps they were waiting for a few more seats to be filled, like a regional bus in Laos. So, they put the passengers up for a night at a hotel on the outskirts of the city, by the airport. They fed us well. Finally, the bus came to pick us up the next day for the airport.

There was a French hippy on the plane who was so excited about going to California and the US for his first time, a journey of his dreams. He was positively giddy. He was a caricature, with his rawhide fringed leather jacket, long hair, 'Make Love Not War' button, a freak flag sewn on the back of his jacket, etc.

Unfortunately, we did not arrive first in Los Angeles, but rather in Duluth, a small city in the far north of Minnesota. We all passed through US Immigration and Customs inspection there. These law-minded conservative civil servants from the high mid-west were not amused by the anachronistic peace-loving hippy. They took him into their little back room. When he came out, he was no longer so excited about his first trip to the US. They apparently did not approve of what they found there. He never made it to California. They kicked him out of the country and back to France.

Being neither hippies nor carrying contraband, we completed our trip without issue. After landing back in Phoenix, I was ready to proceed with the professional phase of my life and complete my MBA. It was also the second time I proved the world is round.

The Gare d'Orsay, Now the Musée d'Orsay

1990

Arizona Desert,
North Carolina Mountains,
And Cowboy Texas

Arizona, North Carolina, And Texas

The 1990 Census

After my second voyage around the world, I returned to finish my MBA at Thunderbird in Arizona. It was September 1989, and I had one semester left. The focus of Thunderbird is completely on global business. There are no US real estate, investing, or insurance classes there, like in most business schools.

One of my classes was an advanced level consulting course. Our client was the state of Zanzibar, an island off the central western coast of Africa and part of Tanzania. Our project was to help them put together a marketing plan for their clove production. Their chief competitor was Indonesia. We did a respectable job with imagination and creativity (clove chewing gum, anyone?). Our client invited us all to visit there after the end of the semester, all expenses paid.

I had a foreign girlfriend living with me at the time. If I had gone, she would have spent Christmas at my mother's house without me. So, I did the right thing and did not go. After wasting many years in a dead-end abusive relationship with her, I regret not going. I will visit there someday. The closest I have been is Mozambique, the country just to the south of Tanzania.

Incredibly, one of my classmates on the project came from Zanzibar. He was part of the large Indian diaspora in Africa. He went to visit his family, of course. Decades later, he contacted me at the beginning of the Covid crisis. He wanted to visit me as he passed through Portugal. Despite his international business education, he became a Buddhist monk. Since he did not believe in vaccinations and masks, I told him I could not meet him. I suppose a properly liberated Buddhist would not be averse to a deadly disease nor cling to a healthy life.

It was December 1989 when I graduated. The Berlin Wall had just come down, and it was the dawn of a new era. Anything was possible. The world was open for me to start my career path. I stayed at my mother's home in the mountains of western North Carolina while I looked for a job worthy of the name. It took much longer than I expected.

With only three things working in my favor, I always had hope. These three were my professional work experience in Hong Kong, many years living overseas, and most importantly, in the end was being fluent in Mandarin. Even so, it would take me seven months to find a job in my career.

Since it was still years before email, I had to use the traditional method of mailing resumes and cover letters to prospective employers. That meant printing hundreds of resumes on high-quality paper at a professional printer. I printed at home on the same high-quality paper my cover letter, tailored to the company and job I was applying for. After all of that, as hard as it is to believe now, I mailed it through the post office with stamps on equally high-quality paper envelopes. The whole process cost far more in terms of money and time than using email.

Computers were expensive then. I bought my first desktop computer, before laptops existed, for my business school needs that cost 2000 US dollars in 1989 dollars. The same today would cost 500 US dollars with far greater abilities. The computer my mother had was so primitive that I had to load the DOS operating system with a floppy disk every time I turned the computer on. It served its purpose.

It was when Microsoft was not so dominant as it is now. Business software was still in open competition. We thought we would always have a choice and that would be fine as long as they were all compatible with each other. For example, I used Lotus 1 2 3, rather than Excel. I used WordPerfect rather than Word. Those days are long gone.

While the job search dragged on, I had to do something worthwhile in the meantime. So, I found odd jobs in the area. I worked in factories on the production line, often during the night shift. This experience helped me later when I was managing large manufacturing operations. I learned what it was like to work 'on the floor'.

Once, I worked for a time in the quality assurance lab of a dental floss factory (of all things). This included pull tests to ensure the strength of the floss in the hands of flossers, etc. One day the factory manager came by while giving a factory tour to a group of visiting Chinese. When I spoke to the group in fluent Mandarin, everyone was suitably shocked.

The year was 1990, and that meant it was the year for the US census, as required by the Constitution every ten years. The census forms had been mailed out, and the deadline for their return had already passed. It was time for the enumerators to spring into action. I joined this august band of brothers and sisters.

Our job was to track down those who did not mail back their forms. So, into the field I ventured with my book of paper maps covering the very rural and mountainous area where the suspects were thought to be. Sometimes a shack was marked on the map in a field with no path to it. I had to investigate. A small group of mobile homes tucked into a remote corner of a mountain had to be checked. No one home? I had to return at night or early morning.

I met an enumerator who worked in an inner city. He told me he had to climb into the abandoned ruins of buildings to find the homeless people who made that their abode. Sometimes he had to crawl in narrow spaces with a flashlight.

Most of the time, people simply forgot about it. Sometimes they found it hidden among a pile of various papers on the kitchen counter. Even if they could not find it, it was of no importance, as I carried plenty of blank ones. I sat next to them and wrote their answers on the many pages form. It was not enough to be counted; they had to answer dozens of questions regarding their lives.

One question always proved the most difficult: their race. The US is an extremely race-obsessed country. The country views everything through the lens of race. It is one of the saddest facts about the US. They had to choose which race they identified as and check the box.

The list started with white, then it continued to African American, then to Latino, then to Asian, and so on to American Indian to Guam (153,000 people with half US military), and finally to American Samoa (50,000 people). Those were the actual words used on the form. At the bottom was a box next to the word 'Other' with an empty line beside it. Very often, people were confused and could not choose their race. It could have been because their parents were Afro-American and Euro-American, or some other mixture. The question asked them to decide their race based on that of either their father or their mother. Today we would use the word 'self-identify'.

Since I could not help them answer, I just patiently waited for them to decide. Usually, they did the sensible thing in an insensible situation. They answered 'American', the only correct answer to that silly question. I wrote that next to 'Other' and checked the box. Interestingly, the question of gender only had two possible answers. It was certainly a different era.

Eventually, The Bombay Company hired me to be their Vice General Manager at the same time they hired a new General Manager for their buying office in Taiwan. I was to be the second in charge of their Asian operations and not the General Manager of Vice. The Bombay Company was an extraordinarily successful furniture and housewares retailer, found in every major mall in the US. The headquarters was in Fort Worth, Texas. Before going to Taiwan, I worked there from July 1990 to January 1991, learning store operations, company culture, products, my colleagues, etc.

Fort Worth is a real cowboy town. It was the endpoint, literally, for the herds of cattle that grazed as far north as Wyoming and Montana. Teams of cowboys herded them there. By the time I lived there in 1990, those days were quickly ending. But the culture lived on.

It was also a military city. McDonnell Douglas had a jet aircraft factory there until Boeing bought them in 1997. The large Carswell Airbase was close to where I lived. When the B-52 strategic bombers took off, they required a long distance before being able to attain any altitude. They did this right over the roof of my apartment. Because I was only living there for some months, I found a cheap apartment in what was once a motel. I had to stop doing everything until the plane flew away.

I became acquainted with all the principal players at the company. One of whom was the Quality Control Manager. I liked him, despite being an excellent example of a Texan 'good ol' boy'. I spent quite a lot of time at the warehouse where the quality control lab was located. Once while we were driving through Fort Worth, he told me that I would see none of them while I lived in Taiwan, implying that would be a good thing. I did not know what he meant by 'them' until he pointed to an Afro-American man standing on the corner. After pondering that obvious factoid for a few moments, I understood his comment and quickly dropped the subject.

Just behind my apartment was a Chinese buffet restaurant. I came to know the Taiwanese couple running it quite well. She was a nurse before. He had a knack for buying depressed, poorly managed Chinese restaurants, turning them around, and selling them for a nice profit before moving on to the next one. These restaurants, usually near big office parks, were extremely popular with office workers on their lunch breaks. The food was good, the service was quick, and the price was reasonable. How could a restaurant like that fail? Incredibly, they did much to his profit. Since he spoke almost no English, I helped him in many ways to improve that restaurant.

While I was living there, a Korean tourist rented an RV (a recreational vehicle or caravan). As he was driving down the highway between Fort Worth and Dallas, he put the large vehicle on cruise control, went back to the kitchen area, and made himself something to eat. He created a terrible accident, blocking the highway for half the day. He had not grasped the limitations of that common function on cars in the US. He thought the RV could drive itself. Though the roads are generally very straight in Texas, it is common on busy highways for pesky cars to drive in front of yours, requiring the use of brakes.

We had daily morning management meetings when we went around the table telling our colleagues what we had done the day before and what we would do for the coming day. Besides learning about the company and its products, I had little to do specifically while I waited to go to Taiwan. Once I volunteered to translate a Japanese article about the company in a newspaper there. I returned with the translation. Someone asked me how good was my translation.

Having learned the Asian culture of being reserved and self-depreciating, I was not yet used to the US corporate culture of bragging and self-aggrandizement. I replied that it was an ok translation, as any Asian would in a similar situation. Their reply to that was, "Then, what good was it?" I had to defend myself by saying it was a perfectly fine translation.

The then current general manager, whom we were replacing, was a woman from Singapore. Once she came to visit the corporate headquarters. She wanted to meet me. We met in an unused office. She sat behind the desk and had replaced the normal chair in front with a short stool. So, during our meeting, she sat high above me. It reminded me of the famous photo of the British officers surrendering Singapore to the conquering Japanese in February 1942. The Brits were forced to sit on short stools while their victors sat in regular chairs, towering above them. Being from Singapore, she knew that photo well. I could only laugh inside.

After all of that, the time came for me to return to Taiwan, a country and culture I was more comfortable with. I was looking forward to a new adventure there. Above all, I was taking more steps on my career path that would take me far.

The Magnificent Grand Canyon

1991

Taiwan

Taiwan 1991 to 1993

Triumphant Return

This next chapter of my life in Taiwan differed greatly from the one before. I returned as the second highest representative of a large US company. I was a decently paid professional working in the dynamic business world of this island nation.

We were located on the central west coast in Taichung, the third largest city in Taiwan. Our responsibility was to manage the new product development, the sourcing, the buying, the manufacturing, the shipping, etc. of most of what The Bombay Company sold. The largest part was overseeing the production of our product at our suppliers' factories.

Bombay's main product line was furniture and other decorative houseware. The style was British of the seventeenth and eighteenth centuries, with a rich, dark cherry finish. Traditionally, the normal finish on furniture in the US market was nitro-cellulose (NC) lacquer, also a major ingredient of gunpowder. It was relatively cheap and easy to apply, but of lower quality. It tended to yellow over time and could be scratched off. A cup with a wet bottom left on a table surface often leaves a white circle. We always had to use coasters, cardboard or wooden squares, that we put our cups on.

We were pioneers in using acid-curing (AC) lacquer in North America, though it was common in northern Europe. This was more expensive and difficult to use. NC lacquer was applied directly. AC lacquer was applied in two parts and had to be cured in ovens. The difference was a much more durable finish without any of the problems mentioned earlier.

The other thing that we were pioneers of was using rubber wood. Rubberwood comes from the rubber tree. Traditionally, when a rubber tree started slowing down its production of rubber, the tree's sap, after about twenty to thirty years, the rubber plantation workers cut down and burned it to make way for a younger generation of trees to take up the hard work. While traveling through rubber plantations in Malaysia and Thailand, one can see them in long, orderly rows by the hundreds.

Instead of burning the trees, we bought the wood at a very reasonable price and used it to make furniture. Today rubberwood is used in most furniture, as any IKEA store shows. The wood is pale white with little personality in terms of grain pattern, unlike oak or pine. So, it is usually painted.

Soon after I arrived, Bombay started a new brand that was managed separately with its own stores. It was called Alex & Ivy. The store design and product concept were similar. The style, however, was North American colonial, which meant it was a lighter colored fruit wood. Fruit wood is the wood of fruit trees. The most common are walnut, cherry, apple, etc. While still using AC lacquer, the color of the finish was much lighter. In both cases, we used rubberwood.

However, we only used rubberwood for chairs, the turned parts such as table legs, and other smaller pieces. For larger surfaces like tabletops and the like, we used Medium Density Fiberboard (MDF). Rather than large pieces of thin wood scrap placed randomly and pressed together with glue like normal fiberboard, MDF uses fine wood particles instead. This makes for a much more durable wood surface, stronger than solid wood and normal fiberboard. Another problem with solid wood is that in different environments, like too humid or too dry, it can warp, which MDF never does. Thin layers of veneer of more expensive wood, such as fruit wood, were used on all visible MDF surfaces to give the furniture more personality.

Besides being second in charge of all company operations in Asia, I was personally responsible for setting up a parallel buying office with all the responsibilities of the Bombay line, but with separate suppliers and my own team. Bombay did not want Alex & Ivy to interfere in any way with its own production. It was a lot of work and responsibility, but I loved it. I drove all over Taiwan in my locally made Ford finding, visiting, and ultimately selling the idea to previously unknown factories of joining this new concept with a bright future, though with much smaller order quantities to begin with. I was extraordinarily successful and am proud of what I achieved.

The office had about thirty employees. My team was just the three of us. We had to do everything except administrative and logistics. We could at least share those functions with the larger office. Ivan was my dedicated Quality Inspector. He was one of the coolest easiest going but most professional Asians I ever worked with. He had a great sense of humor. I genuinely enjoyed working with him. He had a useless, withered arm, which made him unpopular with his compatriots. It never affected his work, and it never bothered me.

I needed a dedicated assembly instructions drawer. While I was walking through a park in central Taichung one day, I saw an Asian woman creating wonderful ink drawings of the natural beauty of the park. I spoke Mandarin to her, which she did not understand. It turned out she was Swedish (!) of Korean descent. I offered her a job. She was outstanding.

One is probably very familiar with the rarely understandable assembly instructions of the ubiquitous ready-to-assemble furniture of today. Though I wrote the instructions, her drawings were literally works of art. Between the two of us, our assembly instructions were truly the best in the industry.

The CEO was Canadian who learned how to do business the US way. With his obnoxious, egotistical arrogance, he would have fit easily in any boardroom in the US. I point this out because he was very unusual for a Canadian, who are generally much less of these things than their US counterparts.

He came to visit us once. He wanted to see our main suppliers. At one such factory, the owner was delayed for some reason, probably because of the terrible traffic. Rather than sit and wait in the meeting room like the rest of us, he petulantly got up and sat in the van. When the owner returned, the CEO made him wait.

We had a breakfast meeting with the General Manager, him, and me, to discuss business in general. The subject of Ivan came up. The overall Quality Control (QC) Manager, a sour, uptight, weaselly character, did not like Ivan for no other reason than his handicapped arm. In the beginning, Ivan officially reported to him, though he already was working with me on the Alex & Ivy line. The CEO probably heard the QC Manager complain about him and asked us what we thought.

What he really wanted to know was should he follow the advice of the QC Manager and fire Ivan. The General Manager did not dare cross his boss, who had apparently already made up his mind. Aghast that the company would fire an excellent employee for no reason (a common practice in US companies), I spoke up and defended Ivan. I offered to take him off the QC Manager's hands to work directly for me on the Alex & Ivy project. He agreed.

Tony was the company driver. He was a simple farmer and beekeeper. We became friends. Visitors from the US head office treated him with great condescension. The CEO was the worst, treating him with slight contempt as the lowly employee that he was, the lowest paid in the entire company.

Ironically, he was also by far the richest in the company. Because of the land prices in Taiwan at the time, he sold enough land to have well over ten million US dollars in cash. I know this because he once asked me for help in applying for US residency based on investment in a US company that produced a certain number of jobs. The minimum investment was ten million US dollars. He took the job because he wanted to practice his English and be around Americans from the US, not for the money.

As a beekeeper, he experimented with honey. He made medicine from honey that cured things such as cold sores inside the mouth and nose, self-inflicted wounds when biting one's tongue, etc. I tried his invention. It worked very effectively on me. Considering the natural properties of honey, there is no doubt in my mind. For example, honey is the only food that never spoils. It naturally prevents any fungus, bacteria, etc. from occurring. So, why would it not be effective with low-level infections like those I mentioned above?

Much of my work involved developing hundreds of new products. The US office sent me large packets of blueprints by mail of these new products, ranging from four-post beds to small tabletop decorations. Since this was before the time of CAD (Computer Aided Design) digital drawings and an email system to send them, we had to use the ancient method of paper drawings which had every dimension and other key information in blue ink on a sheet of paper a square meter/yard or more in size.

The factories quoted their prices based on the drawing. If reasonable, I had them make samples, which I sent to the head office for approval. If all went well, I chose the best factory and placed a production order. During the production phase, I did the drop test of the packaging with a sample, according to specific guidelines to ensure it could survive the trip to the US by ocean freight in a container. I regularly checked the production process and did a formal final quality inspection with my buddy Ivan before shipment.

My apartment was located on a rise off the main road that connected the city to the port on the west coast. It was a newly built three-bedroom apartment with a large terrace and a magnificent view of the city lights to the east. A traditional cemetery immediately occupied the hillside below the apartment building. Most local people would not live so close to a cemetery. I had no problem because it is the living who can harm us and never the dead. Besides, at least one side was silent.

I lived with a Taiwanese girlfriend. We used one of the bedrooms as a walk-in closet. I bought several stand-alone clothes hanging bars, like one sees in clothing stores. I used the other bedroom as a home office. A large US-style washing machine I brought over from the US dominated the small balcony off the kitchen. We still had to dry the clothes by hanging them from a bar hanging from the ceiling of the same balcony, like everyone else. Likewise, the large refrigerator I brought from the US dominated the small kitchen. Both were huge compared to the Taiwanese equivalents.

Once for a few weeks, a hawk lived on the large terrace. He could easily see his prey from that perch above the cemetery. Down the street and on the other side of the main road was an important university in Taiwan, Taichung University. There, I could use the large indoor swimming pool and sprint around the running track.

At the start of the day, I ran along the lonely, quiet lanes of the cemetery connecting all the traditional Chinese sepulchers below my apartment. After work, I did hundred meter/yard sprints on the running track at the university. I rested as I jogged slower around the curve of the track before doing another sprint down the straightaway. Otherwise, I ran around the quiet lanes of the surrounding countryside. I was very physically fit. Every morning before work, I also meditated for an hour.

Once there was a large group of students on a short-term exchange program from the US studying Mandarin at Taichung University. A local pub asked me to be the DJ for a party they had there. So, with my comprehensive collection of cassette tapes of western music, I did so. They loved it, dancing on the pub floor.

Dancing had become legal since I had lived there five years before. It was quite a challenge to queue up individual songs on cassettes. In exchange, the pub gave me free beer. Since the only beer in Taiwan then was Taiwan Beer, that is what I drank. At least it was cold and wet.

I hired a tutor to teach me the local dialect that 80% or more of the local population speak as their native language. Everyone who went to school after Chiang Kai-shek's army fled there in 1947 learned the official language of Mandarin. But it was Hokkien (minnanyu) they speak normally. It is a dialect of Fujian, the Chinese province directly across the Taiwan Strait from where most Taiwanese originally immigrated. I spoke it reasonably well, though I consider it the most difficult of all the dozens of languages I have studied. I did the same with Cantonese ten years later when I worked in Guangdong Province for Black & Decker.

While I was living there, coincidentally, a friend from my time at the University of Chicago was working in the US embassy there. We lived in Taiwan during my first stay, studying Mandarin. We shared an apartment then, too. After many tries, he managed to achieve his dream of a career in the US State Department. He was at the lowest level then, which was processing visas. Later, he rose to important levels in various embassies around the world.

He once invited me to an embassy party, where I met his colleagues. When they asked me what I was doing in Taiwan, I told them the truth that I was working for a US company and was friends with one of their colleagues. Everyone chuckled and did a kind of wink wink nudge nudge with me. I was quite perplexed by that until I learned later that the CIA sends spies under the guise of 'working' for US companies in foreign countries (oh no, was that a state secret?). Ironically, years later, the CIA tried to recruit me twice for exactly that role.

Me Bending Metal Rebar with My Throat Using Qigong in front of the Buddha

Taiwan 1991 to 1993

Enjoying Life in the Business World

This same friend of mine came to visit me in Taichung. We went to a typical local Taiwanese restaurant for lunch, my favorite kind. A man twice our age came out from the kitchen and welcomed us. He spoke English, though it was clear that he had not spoken it in many years. Nonetheless, he spoke it well enough.

I spoke English with him and encouraged him to speak. He told us he had learned English from the US soldiers who were in Taiwan after the end of the Second World War. They taught him how to play baseball. He loved all things and people from that country. The US diplomat refused to speak English with him, pretending he did not understand, causing him to flee back to the kitchen, ashamed of his English.

The next day, I, the 'ugly, arrogant US businessman', returned to that restaurant and found him. I apologized profusely for my compatriot's rudeness, telling him he spoke excellent English and to continue doing so every chance he had. I never have and never will treat anyone with less than the respect they deserve. What position someone holds in an organization, what car they drive, or shoes they wear are never important to me. Ironically, I am more diplomatic than many diplomats.

Taiwanese furniture factories were quite interesting. They used spray booths to spray paint onto the smaller parts of furniture and other items. These consisted of a metal booth about two meters/six feet wide. Water flowed down the front surface of the back wall, which caught the excess spray that did not make it onto the part.

Usually, I saw the spray painter with a lit cigarette hanging from his lips. I made sure I hurried away, as the spray paint with its high percentage of solvents was highly flammable. Of course, goggles were nowhere to be seen.

It was always disconcerting to see a row of prisoners chained together, sitting on small plastic stools, sanding wooden parts, or doing other relatively simple tasks. I suppose it was better than stamping out license plates in US prisons or working on a chain gang picking up trash under the scorching sun along the highways of the US South.

Interestingly, Taiwan was the only country in Asia where I saw women owning and running factories. They usually were found on the factory floors, managing very much with a hands-on approach. There was no question of who was in charge.

Most factories were relatively small, with perhaps only a hundred workers or fewer compared to the thousands found in Chinese, Japanese, or Korean factories. Because of Taiwan's deep manufacturing base, many activities are subcontracted out. Even so, every owner knows intimately their business. They know precisely the number of screws and of what size are required for any item they make. They know what each screw costs. I can think of no other Asian country where this is true.

I became friends with many of the factory owners in my supply base. They took me to visit various places on the weekends. For example, I loved visiting the tea plantations in the mountainous interior of the island. I learned a lot about tea. My favorite place to go for tea was a mountain named Dongding, especially for the spring tea harvested at that time. Tea experts consider the Wulong tea grown there the best in the world.

If you ever see the words Gaofeng Dongding Wulong Cha, 高峰凍頂烏龍茶 (or the equivalent sounding words, as Taiwan does not use China's pinyin system of spelling), try it. I did not like the cheap 'election tea', which political candidates distributed in boxes for free during election campaigns.

Another factory owner gave me organic rice from his farm. Before cooking it, I would need to spread the rice kernels on my kitchen table to remove all the black bugs. I found that eating the few that I missed was no big deal, as they were organic, too.

For a time, I played tennis with another owner and his friends before work. I went on local hikes with another one and his group of friends. Once on a mountain trail, someone in our group ahead of me ate a candy bar and threw the wrapper on the pristine forest trail. I hurried ahead, picked up the wrapper, and handed it to him, telling him that he had dropped something. He understood my meaning.

Others took me and two other friends to play golf on the weekend. Because the courses were usually wrapped around mountains, there were no golf carts. Instead, middle-aged women accompanied us with their wide straw farming hats, carrying our clubs and recommending which one to use at any particular hole, as any caddy would. I doubt they played a round in their lives. I took it seriously then, making sure I spent a few hours at the driving range during the middle of the week. Nonetheless, I could only hit in the middle nineties, despite all the time I invested.

One wealthy factory owner even offered me his daughter's hand in marriage and part-ownership of his company. She was very attractive and kind-hearted. I could have done worse (and did). The main thing that stopped me was her voice. It was a horrible rasp that I could not countenance listening to, the first and last thing of the day for the rest of my life.

During the many religious festivals in Taiwan, factories had large dinner feasts with hundreds of guests. On these occasions, I ate many traditional things that were not commonly found in restaurants. Pork is the most popular meat in Chinese cuisine. I can attest to the fact that they eat every part of the pig, including the naughty bits, except the tail. In traditional food markets (so-called 'wet markets'), it was common to see a full pig's face for sale. I always thought it would make a great Halloween mask.

These religious folk festivals show the very strong Daoist/Taoist influence on society. In contrast to a Buddhist event, most dishes were meat, and alcohol was served without limit. It is normal to see offerings to the spirits with cups of alcohol (baijiu) and plates of pork on the altars of Daoist/Taoist temples.

Alcohol was a big part of doing business in Taiwan. Even now, Taiwanese businessmen have quite a reputation in Asia. I remember factory owners taking me to wonderful Japanese restaurants for lunch, which is one of my favorite cuisines. After a lot of sake, I would make my way back to the office and try to work for the rest of the afternoon. It was often a futile effort. The only other people who are even worse are the business lunches in Ukraine and Russia.

As in Ukraine and Russia, one never picks up a glass and drinks from it on one's own. One must drink with someone else. This means that if one wants to take a sip, one must toast someone else at the table. Did I write 'sip'? No one sips on these occasions. One toasts the other and empties one's glass at one go. After toasting someone in Taiwan, they show the empty bottom of their glass to the others, proving that they are not cheating by not drinking the entire contents. Fortunately, the glasses are usually, though not always, the size of large shot glasses. No one toasts hard alcohol with pint glasses, half pint glasses, maybe.

For many years during this period of my life, I had the dream of entering the US Foreign Service. By this time, I considered myself not only very international but also very diplomatic. The process started with a written exam given at US embassies around the world. I always passed those. That would be followed by an in-person, all-day series of oral assessments and group exercises in the US.

Though I tried a few times, they never accepted me. The system works against Euro-American men. This is no secret. The official policy of the Foreign Service (and every other department of the US federal government) is to give certain groups of people points based on their race and gender. It is called Affirmative Action. For example, an indigenous woman was given the most points. As they worked their way from there to where I was, the points given were fewer. Euro-American women still received extra points due to their gender.

Though it was frustrating, by the time I gave up that quixotic dream, I already had an international career in business that would be highly successful. I was better suited to the (mostly) merit-based world of commerce rather than the world of big government bureaucracy, where I would have to change my point of view as every new administration changed the foreign policies of its predecessor.

While I was working during the day, I found many interesting things to do in the evenings. I took classes in Qigong and Buddhist meditation with a famous Vietnamese monk who had found refuge there from the Marxists of his native country. He and his dozen or so young Taiwanese disciple monks lived in a large flat in Taichung. There, I learned the power of the mind over the body.

Later in our training of Qigong, we could bend rebar with our throats. One classmate held one end of the rebar, while the other placed the other end where the throat meets the shoulder blade under the chin. Then, with great concentration, we exhaled strongly and lunged our necks towards the one holding the other end. We bent it every time.

I bent two dozen or more rebar rods that way. I would not have believed it if I had not done it myself.

If I arrived early, the monks and he sometimes were just finishing up their dinner. Once I noticed that they had eaten a meat dish. I asked him about that, considering the vegetarianism of Buddhism. He replied that he did that occasionally to make the greater point of Buddhism to his disciples. In Buddhism, the goal is to neither have an aversion nor cling to anything. One should always have an equanimous mind. This is the most important part of Buddhist thought. Clinging to rules is a form of clinging, as is clinging to one's beautiful woman, Jaguar, or nice house.

This is why I could never be a Buddhist despite its obvious attractions. I once read in a Buddhist text the advice of what to do when one feels an attraction to a beautiful woman. The advice is to view her as a walking skeleton, or better yet, a rotting cadaver, which is how we will all become in the end anyway. Though I do not cling to a car or a house, I do have a powerful attraction to the woman I love. I prefer her to all others. I do not, nay, I cannot have an equanimous mind to beauty and love. So, a true Buddhist must live as a monk in a remote mountain forest monastery. I will settle on living joyfully in the world of the red dust.

After three years working for Bombay, they told me that they would send me to Malaysia as General Manager to set up the sourcing base there. It was an excellent and natural move for my career. But at the last minute, the Vice President of Store Operations at the Bombay head office, a close friend of the CEO and his Dutch wife, the creative director, wanted the position. They gave it to him, though he had no qualifications for it. Store operations versus creating and managing a manufacturing supply base are not even close. I was fed up with the company for this and many other reasons. No wonder they went bankrupt and closed everything fourteen years later.

I quit. Once that fact was generally known, it did not take long to find another opportunity. Leader Paint was the representative supplier in Taiwan for the huge Dutch industrial coatings company, AkzoNobel, which supplied the acid curing finish (paint) that we specified to the factories. Dickson, the president of the company, hired me to be the General Manager of their production and business operations in Thailand. We had an excellent professional working relationship. We worked well together on the Bombay and Alex & Ivy production. He was one of the coolest Asians I had ever met. I accepted at once. Living and working in Thailand was my next adventure.

Typical Local Temple in Taiwan

1992

Brunei and Sarawak

Brunei and Sarawak 1992

Retired Headhunters

February 1992 was Chinese New Year's in Taiwan. It was three weeks long. I needed to take a well-deserved vacation. I chose to visit a part of Southeast Asia where I had never been, namely the small, oil-rich country of Brunei and Sarawak, Malaysia. Both are on the northern part of the island of Borneo.

Arriving from Hong Kong, I had a surprising amount of complications with my visa. In the end, they gave me a one-week visa, which was more than enough. The Sultan lives in a great modernist palace with Islamic influences by the water. I was told that he was the largest depositor in the Bank of England. Locals also told me that he legally owns everything and everyone in the country.

Brunei is not much more than the city, Bandar Seri Begawan, surrounded by jungle. My impression was that it was surprisingly rundown. Foreigners held most positions in the government administration, including schoolteachers, customs and tax administration, police, military, judges, etc. The army consisted of Nepali Gurkhas of the British army, the same who were based in Hong Kong. The Sultan clearly did not trust his own people to do anything serious.

An expat bar in Taichung invited a few exotic dancers (strippers) from Circle Circle, the most famous such institution in Dallas, Texas. I was there with other business acquaintances. I would never go see such a thing on my own. Why get all hot and bothered with no release? I talked to one of the professional dancers between pole dances. She told me of an experience that she and her colleagues had in Brunei a short time before (on the same tour?).

The Sultan of Brunei hired a plane full of the sweet, young dears from Circle Circle to perform at a private party at his palace for a weekend. They were paid very well by any standard. But there was a misunderstanding, apparently, because they were expected to do more than dance around a pole. They were miffed about that. It should have been spelled out in the contract. It was probably just a case of a lot of alcohol and boys just being boys.

I was glad to leave Brunei, though the rough dirt road to the border was not very pleasant. It was meant to delay any Malaysian invasion from reaching the city by about thirty minutes. My visa complications continued at the border, where they would not issue me an exit permit unless I first had a re-entry permit, only obtainable in Singapore or Kuala Lumpur.

They did not see the remarkable irony that the requirement meant I had to leave the country to do that. I told them I had no intention of ever returning. With their noses a bit out of joint by that statement, they let me go. They probably thought I worked there. The idea that anyone would visit Brunei as a tourist must have been too farfetched.

The small Malaysian border town on the other side was like a breath of fresh air. Most everything was owned by non-religious Chinese, which made the village much livelier than the strictly Muslim city in the distance, hidden by a rainforest.

It took three days and three boat trips west, hopping along the northern coast towards my destination of the city of Kuching (meaning ‘cat’ in Malay), the provincial capital of Sarawak. There is a wonderful museum there dedicated to cats and their role in world culture and art through the ages. Since I adore the subject of the museum, I spent half a day there.

I took a day trip into the forest to hike the trails. There, I came upon a longhouse of the local tribal folk. They invited me in and showed me around. The interior was dark, with cooking fires illuminating the shadows. I was not too far from the influences of the city. The young folk were educated enough to speak English.

Within the longhouse are sections walled off by wooden planks where a family lived. The doors of these private living spaces opened onto a common passage. Common areas for socializing, cooking, and eating fill the remaining space. They are built on stilts with a large, covered veranda wrapping around the exterior. About a dozen families lived in a longhouse. A normal hamlet had four or five such dwellings. The high roofs and the open design allow for plenty of ventilation. The whole design is centered on communal living. Usually, they have neither electricity nor plumbing, just as they have lived for thousands of years.

In many large mesh sacks hanging from the dark corners of the rafters, I could see the smiling visages of skulls all bunched together. I asked the headman, through one of the young English speakers, about them. Sensing my alarm that I was among headhunters, he replied those skulls were from the heads of Japanese soldiers taken during their occupation in the Second World War or from enemies of earlier times. Besides, they stopped hunting heads a while ago. Considering that old habits die hard, I left shortly afterwards.

While working for the Bombay Company, I became associated with the Southeast Asian Wood and Timber Professional Association. I visited their office in Kuching. Borneo is famous for its orangutan ('man of the forest' in Malay) population and is the source of much commercial timber production. I had planned to go upriver to see the logging operations myself, but due to conflicts between the logging companies and the local tribals over money, I decided not to risk being stuck there. Though the locals are paid very well, conflicts are common.

As with most everything in Malaysia and Southeast Asia, the ethnic Chinese control most of the economies. They are descendants of China who arrived several hundred years before. Organizing themselves by clans from their various geographic origins in China, they only marry within the group. Thus, they keep their language and traditional customs alive.

I attended a monthly dinner at a local Chinese restaurant, given by the chairman of the association. The hall was filled with ten large, round tables. Each had ten people sitting around them. Since I spoke Mandarin, worked in the industry, and was (still am) a sympathetic white man, he asked me to sit next to him in the place of honor.

On the other side of him sat another white man, who neither spoke Mandarin nor was in the industry. He was the president of Rémy Martin, famous for its wonderful cognac, visiting his company's biggest private customer. He was not comfortable sitting among relatively uneducated, uncouth (by French standards) timbermen with whom he could not communicate. Yet there he was. Much to his relief, I could translate for him.

You may be as surprised by this situation as he was. I, however, was not. These monthly feasts with, say, a hundred or more Chinese, all drinking the most expensive cognac money could buy, were normal within the world of Asian business associations. No one was sipping their special cognac sniffers. Everyone had a simple 250 ml/8 oz beer glass in front of them, half full. At every toast, everyone at the table, or in the entire room when everyone toasted the chairman, emptied the glass in one gulp. The only way one could drink was by toasting another. No one ever drank on their own.

One toast per table of ten immediately consumed 1250 ml of cognac (10 times 125 ml). That is equal to one and two-thirds of a bottle. Multiply that by ten or more tables and then by the twenty or more toasts each table does through the course of a dinner. The math quickly adds up. Because he is a wealthy head of his organization and Chinese, he must maintain face. So, naturally, everything must be top-notch expensive.

Halfway through dinner, the chairman asked the Frenchman if Rémy Martin kept a special reserve of the best bottles from each year. He replied yes, indeed they do. The chairman asked how much a bottle would cost and how many were there. The Frenchman shook his head, replying that they were not for sale.

The chairman continued his line of questioning. Of course they were not for sale, but in a completely hypothetical world, what price would he put on these special bottles, and how many bottles of the best Rémy Martin were there? The Frenchman patiently replied that they normally keep a thousand bottles of the best, but since they were not available, the point was rather moot.

This went back and forth until the cognac president threw out a price of ten thousand US dollars a bottle. The chairman thanked him, called over his assistant, who returned moments later with a checkbook. The chairman wrote out a check for ten million US dollars right then and handed it to the Frenchman, who could only accept it. And just like that, the deal was done. But imagine how much face the chairman would gain when he served that! It would be priceless!

A few days later, I flew to Kuala Lumpur, the capital of Malaysia. I liked it much better than the first time I visited seven years before, when money was more of a concern. There, I had a meeting with another representative of the Southeast Asian Wood and Timber Professional Association.

Short on time, I tried to hail a taxi, but not one stopped, even without passengers. I was getting desperate. Finally, one stopped close by to let out the passengers. I jumped into the back seat before the taxi could escape me. He panicked and tried to explain with his non-existent English and waving arms that he was not available.

Noticing he was a 'Sino-Malay', I spoke Mandarin to him and told him to relax. He was immediately relieved that we could communicate. While he was taking me to the office in the suburbs, he explained that almost all the taxi drivers were Sino-Malays. Due to miscommunication between one taxi driver and a passenger in the past, word spread like wildfire, and the rest decided they would not take foreigners.

Soon I returned to cold, rainy Taiwan after a week in Hong Kong. My experiences in Borneo were incredible and unforgettable, especially in Sarawak. Even the names are exotic, reminding me how far off the beaten path I would go.

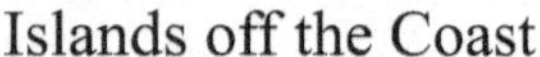

Islands off the Coast

1993

Thailand

Thailand 1993 to 1996

An Attempt on My Life

Thai Leader Paints was located just outside the city of Chonburi, the provincial capital of the province of the same name. It is two hours east of Bangkok by car, on the way to Cambodia. When I lived there, it was a traditional Thai town with most buildings made of wood in the local style. There was no commercial center to speak of. I bought my food at the sprawling, old, open-air market in the center.

I lived with a Taiwanese woman friend in a single-story house surrounded by a yard that was dominated by an enormous mango tree, which produced hundreds of mangoes when in season. As is normal in Thailand, the kitchen and maid's quarters were in a small separate building from the main house. This excellent idea was to keep the hungry insects away from the living quarters.

Not having a maid, I used that small room as my home office. I brought my desktop computer from Taiwan, which I originally had bought in the US. Laptops did not exist yet. I had to buy an electric converter to use with it because of the voltage difference. There were no universal power supply adapters then that all laptops have today. In case you are curious, they are the small black rectangles found on every laptop power cord.

The house itself had two bedrooms, a bathroom, and a living room. We ate our meals in the covered space between the house and the kitchen, where our dining table and chairs were. Down our residential street was another larger two-story house where the company's several Taiwanese technicians lived. The Gulf of Siam was at the other end of the street, visible across a wide, wet mudflat.

It flooded the street sometimes during the rainy season, but since all the houses are built on a foundation about a meter/yard high, the water did not quite reach the living quarters themselves.

Before the internet, ingenious humans invented other ways to communicate over vast differences. In those days, one such method was short-wave radio. They practically do not exist today. But back then, one could listen to BBC broadcasts from London, for example. I particularly enjoyed the BBC radio show of the time that introduced new popular music called Radio 1.

Since my little short-wave radio could only get static, listening to music was not possible. The answer was to string metal wire around the walls of my living room just below the ceiling and connect it to the antenna. By doing that, I received good enough reception so that I could enjoy the music. It was not pretty, but it worked.

Shortly after I arrived, I decided I needed to speak Thai. I hired a young woman as a tutor to teach my woman friend and me the language. This, and working in a world absent of English, made me fluent within a year. The language is tonal, like Mandarin. Since I was a near-native speaker of Mandarin, that was not difficult.

What was difficult was reading. Forget about writing. I learned the alphabet, but the total lack of punctuation and any other indication of sentence breaks (capital letters do not exist) made reading nearly impossible. The difficult alphabet itself has seventy-two letters.

Since Thai is not a literary language, there was not much to read other than newspapers and translations of popular Western bestsellers. Thais did not have a written language until 1283, when the king decided to use the Old Khmer system of writing from neighboring Cambodia, which originally came from southern India, brought by Indian missionaries to Southeast Asia.

Every language has its idiosyncrasies. For example, 'thank you' in Portuguese is 'obrigado' if you are male or 'obrigada' if you are female. In Thai, there often is a word at the end of the sentence used as a gentle form of emphasis. Males use 'Kop' and females use 'Ka'.

In an expensive restaurant in Hong Kong, years after the handover to China in 1997, a Chinese general took a gorgeous, very feminine, young Thai woman to dinner. Clearly, it was a personal business arrangement between the two. English was not their forte. The general said something to her. She laughed too loudly and replied with the word 'Kop' at the end of her sentence. I wonder if the enamored general ever found out the truth of the matter, or if, in the end, he did not care.

Thailand has three seasons of equal length: the rainy (May to September), followed by the dry (September to January), continuing to the wet (January to May) before starting the cycle again. I liked the rainy season because it was much cooler as the clouds blocked the sun and the rain removed the humidity. The dry season was pleasant, too, but as we progressed through it, the terrible heat and humidity of the wet season became ever more oppressive. It always felt strange for the 'winter' to be the hottest time of the year.

A strange thing always happens a few times during the rainy season. After a particularly heavy rain, the phone lines (only landlines, then) became drenched, causing mayhem in the limited world of telephony. If someone called me, someone else across town would answer. The numbers were not jumbled, just unmoored from their fixed place of residence. It took about two weeks for things to return to normal.

Thai Leader Paints was a sleepy little company led by a morose Taiwanese caretaker bureaucrat, who always had a scowl on his face. He did nothing but service the few nearby Taiwanese customers that the company president had established years before. These were factories in Thailand owned and managed by Taiwanese. The Mandarin-speaking office manager was a plump, close-minded Sino-Thai spinster who mothered the seat-warming caretaker like the child she would never have.

The head of production was a fat Taiwanese technician who dominated all things outside of the office. He took to Thailand like a duck to water. He spoke Thai well and had his local mistress living with him to take care of the house and the other Taiwanese living there, including cooking, cleaning, and washing clothes, etc.

There was another Taiwanese technician who had no ambition. He drank too much and could not hold his liquor, as they say. Every time the group of us went out for our weekly dinner, he became falling down drunk and blew his dinner in the back seat as we drove home. Every single time. There was usually another Taiwanese helping for a month or so. Everyone else working there were Thais.

We had many excellent mid-level Thai technicians, delivery drivers, salesmen, and women working in the office in administration and accounting. In all, there were about twenty-five employees. The factory itself occupied half the land available. The other half was a grass-covered field. A high wall surrounded it all, with a guard in a guardhouse at the gate.

There was a small, square concrete building where we stored nitrocellulose, a key ingredient in nitrocellulose lacquer common in traditional furniture finishing. It is also a key ingredient in dynamite. Hence, we stored it in a separate building with a tin roof that was not fixed to the building. So, if it were to blow, the explosion would safely go up rather than sideways. Without that safety valve, an explosion would have turned the building into a bomb with concrete shrapnel killing anyone nearby. With our design, the roof might fly off to a field far away, depending on the wind, but the walls would be intact. Luckily, it never exploded while I was there.

We produced a wide range of industrial coatings for the wood, metal, and ceramic industries. All our customers were other factories. Many of the wooden furniture factories we supplied were suppliers of IKEA. Unlike their counterparts in Taiwan, factories in Thailand were huge, trying to do everything under one roof. At many factories built along rivers, logs entered one end, and finished furniture came out the other.

Another unique aspect of Thai factories of any product is that the workers on the production line were all women. Supervisors, managers, and above were all men. The vast majority of the employees were women. Where were the rest of the lesser educated men? They worked in more physically demanding or unpleasant work, like working with solvents all day in a coatings factory. Otherwise, they were goofing off, living off their women.

A very attractive woman worked in our office. Once a week, her 'man' knocked at the company gate to ask her for money. She always gave him some. She knew he would use it to get boozed up with friends and go whoring, since she paid for all other living expenses. But she thought what could she do? Men were like that. I thought she could have done a lot better, starting with me, for example. Preferring a simple life, I never tried.

We had several drivers, mainly delivering our barrels of product to our customers. They were standard fifty-five-gallon oil drums. Sometimes, they would drive me to visit customers on the rare times I did not drive myself. Often, we had to refuel at petrol stations. I always sat in the back seat, usually busy with something.

Once, on a hunch, I checked the receipt the driver had received from filling up the tank. Since I could see perfectly what the pump showed was the total, it was easy to verify if the receipt was correct or not. The drivers paid for the petrol from an advance they received before they left, and then the office calculated who owed what when they returned. Usually at petrol stations, there were boys of about twelve or thirteen at wooden desks by the pumps who wrote out the receipts. For a few Thai baht, they filled in anything the driver wanted.

I asked him to show me the receipt and, as I suspected, there was a significant difference in the driver's favor. I said nothing about it until after we returned to the office. There I met with him and the office manager. I fired him, not for being a thief, but for not taking care of company assets, thinking this would be less offensive to his sense of pseudo honor, such as it was. I also knew that he might get his revenge somehow. But I could not be afraid of my own safety considering such an egregious crime.

Though I had planned to drive to visit an important customer right after that meeting, I was delayed by an hour or so. When I backed the company car slowly out of the parking space, it could not stop. He had cut the brake line before leaving. The guard saw him but thought he was checking something, as the drivers normally do. If I had left an hour earlier, according to my plan, the brakes would have failed while I was driving down the highway. I hate to think what would have happened if that was the case.

To avoid such temptation for other drivers in the future, I contracted with the owner of a local petrol station. All our drivers would fill up there, and he would bill the company at the end of every month. Problem solved. Sometimes one must be creative in problem solving. To finish this episode, that bastard immediately found another job as a delivery driver the next day. He drove by the factory, honking the truck's horn to make sure we all knew this.

Strange Thai Man Playing with a Large Cobra in front of a Picture of the Taj Mahal

Thailand 1993 to 1996

Police for Tourists and Monks

Regarding the environment, my father taught me at an early age to respect Nature. Usually, my Thai colleagues threw the empty plastic water bottles out of the car window. I put a stop to that, telling them to put the empty bottles on the floor of the car and throw them out when they arrived at their destination. They learned the good sense of that.

A much more serious problem was the waste that came out of the process of making industrial coatings. All factories in the industry use the same process. Coatings are made by mixing various chemicals in large vats. After the batch is made, the vats must be washed with strong solvents to be clean to make the next batch. The solvents used to do this would take on the color of the previous batch. What to do with it?

It pained me to see how they took care of it when I first arrived. That was the purpose of the large, empty field next to the factory. They simply dumped it onto the grass. Being so close to the ocean, the water table was only about a meter/yard below the surface of the ground. Those chemicals went directly into the water table and quickly flowed into the ocean. There was no hazardous waste disposal facility anywhere. It was imperative that I found a way to end this terrible habit.

Once again, my creativity came through. We used to paint our barrels a certain color blue. After we delivered the order to our customer's factory, we went to the back where they stowed empty barrels from their various suppliers. Each supplier could immediately identify their barrels by the color, and so, could take them back to be washed and reused. Making this exact blue required us to make a special batch of it, as we would for any specific color.

After witnessing this for some time, I found out that after cleaning the batches of all the various colors we normally made, the resulting color was a light tan within a small range. So, instead of polluting our field and the ocean, I told the factory workers to use that color to paint our barrels. No one really cared what color they were, only that we could identify and retrieve them from behind the factories. And so we did, ending the serious polluting of the local water table.

It is a common misconception that evil Western corporations go to the developing world in order to exploit and pollute in ways they could never get away with in their home countries. Oh, those evil neo-colonial capitalists!

Compared to local companies doing the same business, Western companies are far better environmental and social citizens. Western companies do not pollute the environment like equivalent local companies do. Western companies always pay their employees better than local companies. Always. Western companies lack the connections with the government that local companies do, not even close. This means that it is much easier for local companies to get away with whatever illegal thing they are doing.

The preferred attitude of Taiwanese companies, for example, was to operate in countries where they could pay off whomever to resolve any problem. This is much more preferable than dealing with lawyers and courts. After all, following the letter of the law does not guarantee there will be no legal problems in the world of petty and grand corruption.

In Thailand, there were various police forces tasked with dealing specifically with various groups. For example, there was the tourist police. They patrolled where the tourists gathered to ease any conflicts or petty crimes that may occur between the locals and them (in both directions). Pattaya is a major tourist resort starting from the days when US soldiers took some R&R (rest and recuperation) time off from the horrors of the Vietnam War. One can imagine what sorts of R&R activities these late teens might have found interesting. I went a few times because some of my Taiwanese customers had condos on the beach there and invited me to visit.

The type of tourists who went there were not the most culturally enlightened. Every photo shop in Thailand had a large photo of the Queen in the window. Back in Pattaya, I was there once on the crowded streets of bars, restaurants, souvenir shops, and yes, photo shops, too. A pair of tipsy Australians walked past a photo shop. One asked the other, "Who is that fat, ugly, old broad I see in every photo shop window?"

Two tourist police officers happened to be nearby and overheard them. They were arrested for lese majesty (Latin for 'injuring royalty'), a serious crime in Thailand. I hope they were merely expelled from the country rather than serve time in prison. I was also surprised that the tourist police could understand their Australian accents.

There was another specialized police force: the monk police. It is quite common for young Thai men to spend a year or two as a Buddhist monk. It is not required, but tradition and parents are powerful forces. In other words, most are not at all dedicated Buddhists to the point of giving everything enjoyable in their late teens. I have seen monks in their saffron robes sitting in front of the most famous house of prostitution in Chonburi, drinking beer and comparing notes of their recent experiences inside. This would have been a case for the monk police.

Society did not consider such behavior scandalous. After all, boys will be boys, and all that. However, there were often scandals involving established and older monks, even head abbots of monasteries with money and young women. In a recent example, a young woman was having paid sex with monks, secretly filming them, and then blackmailing them for more money. How would those who voluntarily live in poverty even have money to pay her?

We can find the answer in the customary practice of all the world's organized religions. Whenever a priest/pastor/minister, a mullah/imam, a rabbi, a Buddhist, or Hindu monk does a traditionally required ritual such as a baptism, a marriage, a funeral, etc. it is customary that the recipients of these services pay them for their troubles. Much of this money stays in the hands of the practitioners and never reaches the general coffers of the church, mosque, synagogue, temple, etc.

It was common for the young monks to get a free lunch from local restaurants, as it is the Buddhist custom for monks to beg for their meals with their traditional brass begging bowls. Thais generously feed them, as they gain good karma from doing so. These simple restaurants had a variety of dishes of the day already prepared, spread out on steam tables keeping them hot. One could choose two, three, or more, and the server would put them on one's plate.

One then paid for each portion of food one ordered before finding a place at a table to sit and eat. There was usually a range from vegetarian to fish to meat choices with a corresponding range of prices. Many monks always tried to choose the most expensive meat dishes. The servers refused, sending them back to the end of the steam table where the least expensive vegetarian dishes were. I saw this countless times. Buddhist monks are supposed to be vegetarians anyway.

It was a common tradition in the countryside to pass property from mother to daughter. If the farming family only had a series of boys until the mother could take it no more, the last boy was given a girl's name, dressed in girlie clothes, and treated like a daughter in every way. Gender roles are not fixed in Thailand.

Transvestites and transgendered people were considered normal. There were special venues in Chonburi for large transvestite performances in the best cabaret fashion. They became particularly popular with Chinese tourists. Thailand was and is an immensely popular destination for Western gay tourists.

I was at a pub in Bangkok with other expat friends. We were standing against the back wall, leaning against a narrow wooden shelf where we could put our drinks. I was standing at the end of the row of us and had an unobstructed view of the entrance.

A group of eight young Thai women came in and occupied the empty space on my other side. They unbuttoned their blouses and were showing their breasts to each other. Each admired the other by feeling them. It then was obvious to me that they were all recently transgendered, showing off their newly minted breasts.

No Thai woman would ever show her breasts in public; not even the legions of prostitutes would do that. They started to rub up against me, testing their effect on a random foreign man, perhaps looking for some action. I became annoyed and moved away. Maybe they thought I was only interested in other men. That would have been ironic.

There was a common joke making the rounds then. I was on a train in Thailand. At a station stop, a beautiful young Thai woman boarded the train. She sat next to me. After a short time, she became very flirtatious with me, even amorous. I kept repeating to myself,

"Don't get an erection! Don't get an erection!" Well, she got an erection.

An elderly woman had a shop in the Chonburi market, selling various dried foods. She had two Siamese male cats that lay about the way cats do. I always stopped by to buy something and say hello to her cats. But once I had to respectfully give the cats some distance. One was giving oral sex to the other. The recipient was obviously enjoying himself. Oh, come on, kitties, really? I did not stay to watch the happy ending. The proprietor was embarrassed by my noticing it. Even many Thai animals are gay.

It was quite common for young men of the lesser educated classes to greet each other by grabbing each other's crotches. At every major street corner there was a group of motorcycle taxis where one could hire a ride to somewhere not too far away, sitting on the back. These guys invariably greeted each other that way. A young, gay Australian who lived near me loved this practice and often hung out with the closest group of these guys. I always had to block any friendly attempt on my private parts.

Large tents with garish lights cropped up at night along the main roads leading into the city. They were restaurants serving traditional Thai fare with local beer. Under the tents were long tables with benches. They all disappeared early the next day. I took my salesmen and factory technicians to dinner at a nearby one, usually once a week.

On one such occasion, we consumed a lot of beer, as usual. My main salesman was quite inebriated and unsteadily wandered to the restrooms. He came back shortly after with urine all down the front of his pants. He was somewhat more sober by then. I asked him what had happened. He sheepishly explained that as he stood in front of the urinal, he pulled down his fly, grabbed his thumb by mistake, and let loose. We had to call it a night after that.

Metaphorical Holy Cobras

1994

Thailand

Thailand 1993 to 1996

Monkeys Will Be Monkeys

For the Taiwanese technicians, we went to a seaside seafood restaurant in the nearby town of Sri Racha, the name of the famous hot sauce made in a factory in Los Angeles by a Vietnamese entrepreneur. The town is famous for its stone carvers. There was a row of restaurants, but we always went to the same one. They were outside the town with tall hills across the street. A temple dedicated to monkeys was on the summit.

The long tables were on an open air veranda covered by a metal roof. We ordered all manner of seafood, with the plates covering the table in front of us. Often the monkeys from the temple came down to raid the restaurants. They came by the dozens, leaping and chattering onto the tables. They grabbed whatever they wanted off our plates. If we protested, they threatened us with violence. Even the restaurant staff were afraid to deal with them.

Regarding monkeys, there is a snake temple north of Bangkok full of cobras caged off from their supplicants. There are pleasant grounds surrounding it. On the left side is a large tree full of older married monkeys with their babes all perched up in the branches. On the right side was another tree under which the adolescent male monkeys gathered.

I would not have believed it if I had not seen it myself. Six of these bored monkeys found a puppy. They formed a line behind the dog. They grabbed it by the flanks and held its back legs in place with their own. One by one, they raped the young dog. The puppy was looking about with a surprised look and his tongue wagging out of its mouth. I cannot say it was having a bad time.

After they all had their turn, they looked around for something else to amuse them. They found a cat. They tried the same thing but were in for a surprise. The cat was having none of the strange play. It twisted around and scratched the face of its assailant. They all scampered away from such a prickly ingrate.

Because of experiences like these, the one in the trees above the Tantric Buddhist temple in Nepal, another one I witnessed at the botanical garden in Hong Kong too offensive even for me to print, plus many others, I must say monkeys are not my favorite animal. I would not go as far as the elderly fruit brandy specialist I met in Taiwan, who lived in the secluded mountains and hung their skulls from his rafters after having eaten them. Suffice it to say, I dislike them.

Another salesman came from a wealthy family. He worked with us, not for the money, but to work with an American from the US, who was rare outside of Bangkok. He was quite a character. Every Monday morning, he arrived at work with his hands cut up and bandaged. He was a practitioner of the traditional Thai sport of kite fighting.

How do kites fight, you may wonder? Well, I shall explain. They gather in a park with a large open space. They use normal kites, except for the strings that connect them to their owners. All along these strings, the owners tied broken bits of glass. The object is to try to maneuver one's kite to cut the strings of one's competitors with these glass encrusted strings, releasing the enemy kite into the windy wilds. Of course, handling these strings is hazardous, perhaps more so for the human competitors than for the enemy kites.

There was a small park near where I lived that had a market for snacks and other interesting things. Sometimes there were doctors and nurses giving free blood pressure checks and the like. I had my blood pressure checked by a doctor. It was always on the low side (in those days). I asked the doctor what I should do about it. He seriously suggested I take up smoking. I agreed it would work, but there may be other undesired side effects.

Sometimes at the same market, quacks were there selling one miracle cure or another. Their wild claims were absurd. On rare occasions, charlatans set up shop. I saw one who made a big show with the 'corpse' he had laid out on the grass with a sheet over it. He lifted the sheet, and the 'corpse' certainly was not looking well. After a complicated ritual, he resurrected his accomplice from the dead. That caused quite a stir among the crowd. He passed the hat for his 'performance'. More importantly, he passed his business card out to anyone who might want to use this or other related services.

Mentioning impromptu medical services in the park, I must admit that the formal healthcare system of Thailand was and is far superior to what passes as healthcare in the US, for example. Everyone working person was assigned to their local hospital, which was vertically integrated with almost every special branch of medicine represented. The service was free. Everyone paid a very small percentage of their salary into the system. I paid less than two percent of my salary, which was at the top of the scale. Most workers paid the equivalent of a few dollars per month or less.

Unfortunately, I had the chance to experience this wonderful system personally. My kite fighting salesman drove me out to visit a customer's factory once. He parked near the factory gate. As I rose while exiting the car, I scraped my head against the metal part extending from the door used to receive the padlock to lock it. I felt nothing unusual. But when my salesman looked at me, he knew he had to take me to the nearest medical clinic at once. Though I did not feel any pain, I had cut my head seriously.

The nearest medical clinic was in the middle of a rice field in a small bamboo building. There, a doctor sewed me up with seven stitches. As he did that, I could see a farmer plowing the field through the narrow space between the bamboo slats that made up the walls. The hospital in Chonburi gave me all the follow-up medical care and medicine I needed. Everything was free, including the medicine. I had to ask myself the obvious. If a third-world country like Thailand in the early 1990's could offer universal healthcare, why could/can the US not? It is all about priorities.

The word 'corruption' can be used in many contexts, as corruption occurs in every country in the world. But calling a country 'corrupt' means corruption is pervasive at all levels of society and not at certain instances with a few politicians. Thailand is a 'corrupt' country, as are most countries in the developing world.

First, I shall describe how the police operate. I drove all over Thailand in our low-cost company cars and pickups, visiting customers and even sometimes delivering their orders. I knew where all the speed traps were around Chonburi and made sure I was well below the speed limit before they could see me. They stopped me every time anyway.

I had to read the low-level policeman quickly as there was no way I could hide the fact that I was a wealthier foreigner. For some, if I spoke Thai with them, they found it easier to demand money. For others, they were impressed that a foreigner gave them enough respect to learn their language and would let me go. On the rare occasions they tried to speak English with me, I would always praise their English profusely. This made them happy, and in that warm glow would let me go.

I became exceptionally good at it. If I had to pay when I stopped on the country roads, it was usually 100 baht, about 2.50 US dollars. Interestingly, they only stopped us low cost vehicles, while letting the speeding expensive cars pass. After all, a smaller thief would never try to rob a greater thief.

While I was living there, a typically Thai thing happened. Someone dressed in a police uniform stationed himself at a busy intersection in Bangkok, where the normal shakedown fee was 500 baht, or 12.50 US dollars. He had been collecting his informal road tax for over a month. He was finally caught when a real police car drove by, and he saluted them with his left hand.

A police captain lived in a nice house at the beginning of the street where I lived. He had several expensive imported cars (with import duty over 100%) parked in his front yard space. Every time I passed there were four or five young women washing them. Alas, they were not wearing wet T-shirts. Now you may ask, how could he have all this on his police captain's salary of about 8000 US dollars a year?

I shall explain as it was explained to me. The police force operates like a pyramid marketing company. The lowly police corporal collecting the 100 baht from passing pickup trucks on a country road kept, say, 10 baht and passed the rest up to his superior, who did the same all the way to the police general at the very top. Imagine if every day only 10 baht made it to his desk after everyone in between took his cut, but multiply that by 100,000's of lowly police corporals; that is a lot of money.

Despite that, the career most desirable by Thai parents for their children was not in the police force. It was a job in the Customs Department. That was where the real money was to be made. I knew a Taiwanese factory owner who gave an imported European luxury car to the officer in charge of his import duty payments. He figured the 250,000 US dollars was worth it.

We had to import a container of special chemicals, dyes, and solvents every month to support our production. It was the exact same shipment every time. And every time I had to visit the Customs office at the port where our container was being held to negotiate how much duty we had to pay this time. The official duty rate never changed, nor did the imported product. Hours passed drinking coffee and chatting niceties until he finally got around to telling me how much we owed. It was always much higher than the duty rate should have been. One can guess where the difference went. It was a strange little ritual.

Ah, but one may interject that these are all examples of corrupt officials. So, now we continue to other sides of society. As I mentioned earlier, most Thai manufacturing companies are relatively large, with often over a thousand workers. They strive to be as vertically integrated as possible, with as many production steps done in house as feasible. The owner/CEO visited his office one afternoon out of the week to check on things, mostly to sign checks and have a glance at the accounts. Unlike their Taiwanese counterparts with their much smaller factories, they knew extraordinarily little, literally, about the nuts and bolts of their business. They spent the rest of their weeks managing their real estate dealings, playing golf, and dallying with their mistresses.

A Taiwanese furniture owner, for example, could say how many screws went into any particular table they were producing and how much each screw cost. Their Thai equivalent had no idea. This opened the way for incredible corruption from one end of the factory to the other. Everyone who was responsible for the purchase and quality control of outside components had a hand in the till. We had to play along, too. This was never a problem with our Taiwanese customers.

In many factories, we had to pay the purchasing manager of our coatings a percentage of every order, or he would change suppliers. We also had to pay the quality control manager of our coatings a percentage of every order so that he would not suddenly stop the use of our product for 'quality' reasons. That was bad enough.

Even the accountants were a part of it. It was common for suppliers to give thirty-day payment terms to customers. It was also common that customers would not pay for six months or longer. This was a severe problem with cash flow, the lifeblood of every company. Suppliers were basically financing the businesses of their much larger customers. I tried to apply internal pressure to pay on time by telling the corrupt purchasing and quality leaches that we could not pay them until their company paid us. They would not accept those reasonable terms.

These factories were all suffering from so many parasites sucking away at the bloodline of the company. I spent much of my time chasing down very late payments from our customers. Accountants had the power to put which checks in front of the owner to sign and which ones to postpone until a later date. Ours usually fell into the second category. I asked them what could be done. The answer was for me to pay them ten percent of the invoice, and they would immediately process it for payment.

Bangkok Palace, the Coolest Palace in the World

Thailand 1993 to 1996

Time in Jail

One day, while I was at our factory, two young policemen arrived (on one motorcycle) and wanted to talk about our business operations. As good as my Thai was, it was not good enough to take on subtle negotiations with the police. I told them to wait until the office manager returned from the bank. It would be several hours before she could.

By this time, there were a dozen of them spread throughout the factory. They asked the workers many questions. If I had simply paid off whatever the first two wanted, the problem would not have become so big. The crux of it was that the foreigners working there, three Taiwanese technicians and me, could not produce work permits. We were working illegally; despite the fact we had applied for them months before. In my case, mine should have been approved six months earlier. One Taiwanese technician had just arrived that week.

They took us to the downtown jail. One of our drivers had to drive a company car as they did not have enough space for us in theirs. The lockup consisted of two cells next to each other: one for the women and another, much more crowded one for the men. Both cell doors were open, and prisoners wandered between the two. We sat on the floor in the walking space between the cells. Separating all of this was another wall of bars with a locked door to the main part of the station.

Someone who is called a 'turnkey' managed the locked cell door. He is a prisoner himself, but for whatever reason the jail keepers give him a key to the locked jail door. If the police need to talk to a certain prisoner, he would go and retrieve him from inside the cell. He and I were the only non-Asians there. I chatted with him. He was from Dubai, doing some kind of business in Thailand that went awry because of something his brother did. He spoke quite good Thai.

This was a jail and not a prison. The difference between the two is that a jail is for those waiting for trial. A prison is where they go if things do not turn out well. Another difference between Thai jails and prisons is that jails do not provide meals, just a space of concrete to sit and sleep on and unforgiving steel bars. Relatives and friends must deliver food to an inmate. We saw how that process went as the police took the tastier morsels for themselves before allowing the rest to the intended recipient. A trial could be many months away. Clearly, we could not stay there for that long, even with the company feeding us.

Sure enough, our local Taiwanese Business Council came to the rescue four hours later. I never knew how much the discrete payment was to the Chonburi police chief. However, to add insult to injury, a few members of the Council took us and the police chief to an expensive dinner at the best house of prostitution in Chonburi (where the beer drinking monks had visited). He was quite jolly, with no hard feelings and all that. He had a wonderful meal, a lot of good booze, and a young maiden at the end, all paid for by our local Taiwanese business community. We were not in a jolly frame of mind.

A curious aspect of that special restaurant was the large, glassed area where the young girls sat, each with a number pinned to her ample chest. It reminded me of a large fishbowl. A client would peruse the colorful fish and choose one by number.

The next day I went to the immigration office to demand my work permit. They let me discuss it with the director. He was all smiles, finding the humor in my predicament. Opening his desk drawer, he handed it to me. He had approved it three months earlier, but for unknown reasons it never made its way into my hands. He shrugged his shoulders and gave me the typical half-hearted apology of 'this is Thailand'. If he expected me to pay an informal transaction fee, he should have told me earlier. But he did not ask for any. Perhaps he thought I had already paid enough by being hassled so badly. I was, in fact, working legally when the police raided our factory.

A few weeks later, we had our day in court to be sentenced for our crime. I showed the judge my work permit dated before our arrest and explained that the Immigration office just had not given it to me. That evidence had no effect on him. The four of us stood in a line in front of the judge to be sentenced. He fined us 500 baht each (the amount a driver in Bangkok would pay for his informal traffic fine) and let us go. It was quite an unpleasant experience. It was too much for the technician, who had just been there a few days before being arrested. He quickly returned to Taiwan.

To understand Thailand, it is vital to understand the role of the Sino-Thais in society. Unlike in the rest of Southeast Asia, they all have Thai names, as was required by the 1913 Thai Nationality Act. They all speak Thai as well. But these are the only two things they have in common with their non-Sino-Thai compatriots. Besides being clearly of a lighter skin color, making them easy to spot, they maintain their ties with their family clan, culture, and language. Part of this culture is to place a high value on education and the ambition to succeed, usually through business. They also tend to only marry within their ethnicity. They represent less than 14% of the population.

As with the rest of Southeast Asia, they control most of the economy. Post-war socialist Vietnam is the exception, since it expelled the Sino-Vietnamese in 1979. Every factory owner I met was of Chinese ancestry. Besides business, Sino-Thais control politics. All the modern prime ministers and representatives in Parliament are of Chinese ancestry. There may be exceptions, but I cannot think of any.

So, what do the indigenous Thais control? The answer is everything else, namely the bureaucracy, police, military, and most important of all, the monarchy. The King tries to remain above the fray, but sometimes he must step in. When the corrupt politicians step out of bounds, the generals petition the King to let them take over. If he agrees, a military coup occurs. When the corrupt generals step out of bounds, the politicians petition the King to allow them to return to power and try again. If he agrees, the generals will allow a quick election, and power is returned to the politicians.

As I mentioned earlier, the greatest ambition Thai parents have for their children is to be the head of Customs or another lucrative bureaucratic position. For Sino-Thai parents, their ambition would be success in business and, in addition, perhaps being Prime Minister one day.

One of my customers was the acting head of his factory, being a son of the retired patriarch. He took a liking to me as we were about the same age. He invited me many times to visit the family's country estate. What I found unusual about it was that instead of watchdogs, the family had a flock of watch peacocks. They explained that peacocks were better because they were more sensitive to intruders than dogs. I can say they are much more impressive to look at.

Another interesting trait of Thais is their preference for whisky as their drink of choice. But they do not drink it neat, like I do. Drinking whisky with a Thai included the following: a big container of ice, a bottle of whisky, glasses, soda water, and many times a mixer. The mixer is the concoction that Thai truck drivers used to stay awake. They are sold in small bottles. It is the origin of Red Bull, according to the company's founder.

The waiter always asks how many caps one wants. Whisky is poured in after a tall glass is filled with ice, soda water, and maybe that odd mixer. The 'caps' the waiter refers to is how many whisky bottle caps of whisky does one want? Usually, the answer was two or three caps. To a whisky swigging man who grew up in Philadelphia, that was absurd. A few caps of whisky barely give any color to the drink, not to mention any taste. True boozing was left to my Taiwanese colleagues and customers.

One of the benefits of running an industrial coatings factory was learning how to mix colors to reproduce a customer's color sample. Starting from the basic premise of how colors are perceived by the eye, one learns that colors come from a combination of just three primary colors: red, blue, and yellow. Mixing red and yellow makes orange, red and blue makes purple, blue and yellow makes green.

The millions of distinct colors the human eye can distinguish are a combination of these three colors. The differences are made from a little more of one of the primary colors than the other. More red than yellow makes a deeper orange, etc. For example, I could tell a color mixer that his results need a few more milliliters of red to match the customer's color sample.

Despite Thai Tourism propaganda, Thais are not the 'most smiling' people of Asia. That title goes without a doubt to the Filipinos. Thais are easy-going in general but can be surprisingly uptight about certain things. For example, in every living room, in every restaurant, in every office, etc., a photo of the King hangs framed on the wall. Thais consider it shockingly offensive when sitting to point one's foot at the King's photo. When crossing one's legs in such a situation, be aware of where one's foot is pointing.

Another example is touching the head, the holiest part of the body. Once, a young woman came up to me with her babe in arms. It was a cute baby, so I reached out to pat it on its head. She swung away and fled in panic. Many young women flirted with me while holding their babies for protection, thinking they could do so safely. Indeed, they were safe.

On the street where I lived was a pack of feral dogs. The locals fortunately fed them, so they were not dangerous. It was interesting to watch their social interaction. The alpha male was obvious. He mounted any new male dog to the pack to make clear who was the alpha and who was the omega.

As an example of stark contrast, in our neighborhood lived an alpha cat. There was no pack of cats. Nonetheless, he ruled the neighborhood. The dogs were smart enough to leave him alone. He was an enormous cat of some age, with scars all over his face and body from the many challenges he had to face down to maintain his position in the realm. He walked along the top of the walls that separated the houses. That is how we became acquainted.

People fed the feral cats too, including me. I called him the King, making sure there were no tourist police around. Sometime later, a kitten of about six months appeared on the scene. Being too new to the world, he was not aware of the importance of the King. Rather than fear him, the kitten often came right up to him to try to rub noses and be friends. The old warrior was nonplussed by this act of friendship. Over time, he reluctantly accepted the little one.

One morning I came out to eat breakfast, and laying on the concrete floor was an enormous rat. What made this rat unusual was that it was cut cleanly in half in the middle, as if by a cleaver. Clearly, it was the work of the King. I appreciated his offering of friendship. After this, he allowed me to pet him, rough scars and all.

Besides Buddhism and a Muslim population to the south near Malaysia, there is another religion in Thailand. It is a devotion to the god of the durian, a most bizarre fruit. When the first durians appear for sale on the sides of country roads, Thais become surprisingly emotional and are filled with an uncontrollable desire for this strange fruit.

The fruit, when ripe, looks like a spiked green rugby ball. When opened, the creamy white fruit emits the most offensive stench. I liken the fruit to putrid meat growing on trees. If I were unlucky enough to be caught by surprise while driving with my Thai colleagues at this season, I suffered immensely. They filled the back of the pickup truck with durians and then brought one or two into the cabin and ate them. The stench from their breath was so terrible that the only way to combat it was to eat it too, so I know it well. Even unopened, it stinks so badly that airlines and hotels forbid it.

Boat Market

Thailand 1993 to 1996

How To Open a Bottle of Wine Without a Corkscrew

Once, I had hoped to share my earlier experience of visiting the northern hill tribes with my woman friend. The changes over the ten years since I had made my trek to visit them were incredible. The hill tribes were by then connected by dirt roads to the rest of the country. There was no need to trek for half a day along narrow, overgrown trails to visit a hamlet without running water or electricity. They had running water, electricity, and televisions. They had become thoroughly Siamized.

We were an international group of tourists from various countries. They made dinner for us of their local cuisine. Afterwards, they performed traditional dances and songs for us. It was a thorough tourist experience. Then, it was our turn, one by one, to sing a traditional folk song from our countries. We all did our best in the spirit of the event.

The French sang folk songs of their country, the Germans of theirs, the Japanese of theirs, etc. When it was my time, I stood on the stage and, as with all my fellow foreigners, I announced the country I came from. But as soon as I told them I was from the US, the entire village erupted in a request for a Michael Jackson song. That I absolutely would not do. So, much to their disappointment, I sang the song I had intended to share: Lead Belly's 'The Midnight Special'. That old blues song is as best an example of a US folk song as there is. Michael Jackson?!? Oh, how the times had changed!

As with many other countries in the world, they drive on the left side of the road in Thailand. They do the same in Japan, Hong Kong, Malaysia, Singapore, Indonesia, and Brunei. Burma used to drive on the left side, too. But after independence from the British, they changed to the right side just to spite their former oppressors.

In countries that drive on the left, the steering wheel is on the right side. I drove all across Thailand for over three years. Every time I sat in the driver's seat, my right hand instinctively reached across my chest for the seat belt, as I would when driving a car where the steering wheel was on the left side (as in the US and most of Europe). My hand would not find a seat belt there. After realizing my mistake yet again, I would reach with my left hand to grab the seat belt where it actually was. Any Thai riding in the car with me thought it was some sort of strange religious ritual to avoid accidents or other bad luck.

One of my customers was a crazy Corsican who had the great fortune (literally) to sweep a wealthy Sino-Thai girl off her feet while she was studying in Paris and married her. He returned with her to Thailand, where her father set him up in a relatively modest, manageable wooden furniture factory. We became friends. I spent many weekends at their home in Bangkok.

We never ate before 2200, so I knew I had to eat something around 1800 to survive until then. He cooked his Corsican cuisine quite well, with copious amounts of wine before finishing the meal with whisky. Afterwards, we and other French friends went out to the bars, not returning to his home until 0400. One of those bars was where I met the transgendered showing off their brand-new breasts to each other right next to me.

He was quite a character, to say the least. He showed me various ways to open a wine bottle in the unlucky event of being without a corkscrew. If one is wearing something heavy, like boots, one can tap the bottom of the bottle with the heel of the boot slowly until the cork slides out of the bottle's neck. Without a good solid heel, another method is to swiftly knock the bottle's neck against a hard surface, breaking it off. Just remember not to drink to the bottom of the bottle where the broken glass has settled.

Not being satisfied with our sales, I tried to incentivize the salesmen by giving them commissions. They refused, even though I explained they would never receive less than their current salary, only more. They refused because they disliked adding competition to their merry band. Even my best salesman who would have earned much more, was against the idea.

I encountered this example of cultural differences as president of a US manufacturing company with factories in China about twenty years later. To improve manufacturing operations. I sought help from the experts, the workers actually doing the work. I offered anyone one percent of the annual savings from any recommendation they offered. Some suggestions netted a 1,000 US dollars bonus and a few even over 10,000 US dollars.

Though I knew exactly who came up with the idea, the individual would never accept credit for it. He would say it was the idea of the entire production team. I had to divide it among all of them. Like the Thais, the Chinese did not want to stand out from their group. It is an excellent example of the Asian preference to identify with a group rather than Western individualism, even if serious money is involved.

I successfully turned the failing company around, making it profitable with higher sales. With my typical creativity and imagination, I realized that all of us industrial coatings suppliers were doing the same thing. We were selling a commodity that was sold on price. Cutting prices could only go so far. Offering better credit terms was meaningless when the customer could pay whenever he wanted without repercussion.

How could I change the business model? I decided we were not selling a commodity but a service. We were not selling screws or lumber. Our coatings required the most complicated process of the entire production and added most of the value to the product. The first thing the customer's quality inspector did was pull out his color board and compare it with the finished product before it was packed up and shipped. It was not just the color that was important, but also the sheen (matte or gloss), the adhesion to the substrate, and other attributes.

It was quite common to see behind furniture factories a team of workers trying to wash off the incorrect coating with powerful solvents. Besides the time and expense of correcting the mistake, shipping late always made a customer angry. Noticing this, I turned the industry on its head.

My proposal to customers was simple. We would guarantee that the production run would pass the color board inspection. I would post one of our technicians on the line. He would have everything required to correct any problems in his truck. The customer needed to give him the power to stop the line at the first sign of a problem. It was that simple. Of course, I had to charge higher prices for this peace of mind. Instantly, I broke the downward cycle of ever lower prices.

The normal practice before was to deliver the coatings order to the customer and leave. If the customer noticed a problem or, even worse, the end customer's quality inspector noticed a problem, the supplier would send a technician to ascertain what was the matter and decide what to do. It might take a few days to send one out to the customer and then another day or two to correct the problem at the coatings factory. A week or more could pass before the factory could resume final production. My customers loved me and were happy to pay significantly higher prices.

Most people enjoy Thai cuisine as found in the local restaurants where they live. I too adore it, but I ate a cuisine significantly different from that found in the West. I ate Thai food two meals a day for over three years. The first thing I must mention is that in Asia, except for the Chinese, breakfast does not differ from the other two meals of the day. Breakfast is usually warmed up leftovers from dinner. I took care of breakfast as I am used to before leaving for work.

It was Thai for lunch and dinner. I usually ate at simple local restaurants. Most everyone is familiar with the wonderful Pad Thai, but what about Pad See Ew, Rat Na, Pad Kee Mao, Khao Soi, Nam Ngiao, etc.? Unlike the much more complex Indian curries, Thai curries are simpler, preferring to bludgeon one with strong, spicy hot flavors.

The flavors were of three types: sour (vinegar), salty (fish sauce), and spicy hot (chili peppers, fresh, dried, or a paste). I had to tell the cook how much of these three to put in my order. Since the cooking was done next to where people sat and ate, it was quite easy once I learned how to say it all in Thai. My meal came out perfectly every time.

Besides these dishes, most foreigners have never tried other Thai delicacies. At train stations, vendors walked past the open windows of the passengers who were continuing their journey with open baskets of spicy barbequed grasshoppers. I hated it when the legs got stuck between my teeth. But I enjoyed bamboo worms immensely. As their name suggests, they are found inside their favorite food source.

They are the size of one's middle finger. Their bodies are white when they are fresh (still living) with black heads. One must cook them shortly after buying them at the food market. They are not meant to be saved in the refrigerator. One fries them in oil like French fries. After which they turn golden brown. They taste wonderful, like high protein fries.

An essential part of my mental makeup is to give everyone the respect and human dignity we all deserve. It makes no difference to me the shoes one wears or the car one drives, or even one's position in society. I respected everyone in a company, from the lowliest cleaning woman and gate guard to the CEO and owner.

This often helped me. Usually, I had to visit the CEO/owner during the few hours he was in the office to chase down late payments. I always made an appointment. But usually, he never showed up. No one knew his schedule or whereabouts. I spent many hours waiting for him. It was usually another waste of time.

After I came to know the gate guards, the problem was solved. They always asked me to sign in and with whom I was visiting. But after I regularly stopped and chatted with them, over time, they came to trust and like me. Once they knew I was there to visit the CEO, they told me things such as, "oh, he is not in today. He is busy playing golf with his friends in Pattaya. He will be here next Tuesday morning, as he has a meeting with the bank at 0900." So, I then turned the car around and returned the next Tuesday after his meeting with the bank. For security reasons, the guards knew his schedule better than anyone working in his office.

I had the same attitude toward everyone who worked at my company. When I announced I was leaving, many cried, including grown men. This has happened at various times in my professional career in Asia. How did I manage to receive this reaction? I treated everyone with kindness and respect, not with the meaningless and condescending phrase "we are all one big family/team/partners" like they do in most US companies.

Whenever a baby was born to an employee's family, I was present at the Buddhist ceremony at the local temple. I was there at every wedding feast and every funeral ritual for any close family member of an employee. Yes, it meant that I spent a lot of my personal time at these life events, but I knew how much it meant to them for me to be there. Though I had no expectation of anything in return, they repaid me with loyalty and devotion.

I also must add that when an employee obviously had a serious attitude problem that would not change, I never hesitated in setting them free to find a better work environment (i.e., fire them). For any other reason, I would find another position that was more appropriate for their skills and experience. I made sure everyone always had the proper tools to do their jobs. Except for attitude problems, it usually is the fault of management if an employee is struggling.

A friend of the company president in Taiwan persuaded him to hire a technician from Singapore to work in our Thailand factory. He had worked for many other coatings companies in China and other Asian countries. He had the typical air of superiority that many Singaporeans have and treated all the Thais with condescension. No surprise there.

A week or so after he arrived, one of our best Taiwanese customers had a problem with our coatings. The color was off. So, I sent our new hotshot technician to correct it. Hours later, our impatient customer called and angrily demanded that we do something. Our Singaporean technician was struggling to correct the color. This occurred before I changed our business model.

I sent our best Thai technician there. He quickly adjusted the color, and the factory was back running within half an hour. After they returned to our factory, I asked the Singaporean to mix a few basic colors in front of me. He was not even close. Finally, realizing that his time was up, he admitted that he was colorblind! He had fooled many employers for as long as he could before being found out after only a week or two. Then, he moved on and found his next gullible employer. He must have thought it was all great fun; otherwise, I could not imagine why he chose work that he obviously was incapable of doing.

My experience during my second time in Thailand differed greatly from the first visit as a tourist. Despite all the challenges of running a company there, I greatly enjoyed my time. I left the company in a much better state than I had found it. I left the country a changed and better man than when I arrived.

Working Elephants

1995

Nepal And India

Nepal 1995

Eight Years Later

At the end of October 1995, I returned to Nepal eight years after my first visit there, right after leaving Thai Leader Paints to show my girlfriend at the time. Rather than take the long way through China and Tibet as I did in 1987, we flew directly from Bangkok to Kathmandu. It was the same Nepal on the surface as I remembered, but that was soon to change.

The stability of the country had changed dramatically by this time. Although Nepal changed from an absolute monarchy to a constitutional one in 1990, a Maoist guerrilla war started in 1996. In 2001, according to the official account, the Crown Prince massacred his parents and seven other members of the royal family at a family dinner. Afterwards, he put a bullet in his own head. He died three days later, and his uncle, who was not present, ascended the throne.

Citing the security situation because of the Maoists, he suspended the constitution, declared martial law, and took direct control of the country. In 2006, a mass movement of the People forced him to reinstate the constitution and the national legislature, which ended the civil war. The new legislature suspended all the king's power in 2007 and abolished the monarchy altogether in 2008. This caused the world to lose one of its monarchies. When will the rest of these anachronisms go?

We received fifteen-day visas at the airport. The first thing I did was go to the Indian embassy to get our visas. This was a typical example of absurd, Kafkaesque bureaucracy. We had to waste a morning standing in line at 'Window B' only to fill out a form to be telexed to the Indian Embassy in our home countries to confirm if we really were citizens of the country our passports claimed we were. I have no idea how those embassies could prove that. They probably just returned the telex with a quick check of the box.

For the edification of our younger readers, a telex (teleprinter exchange service) was a system for sending and receiving printed communications before fax (Google that one) and email. It operated through a dedicated phone line between two places, for example, the Indian embassies in Nepal and the US. The message was printed out as it could not be saved to be read later. It had no memory.

After five to seven working days, they would post a list of those verified by their respected home Indian embassies. Only then would the visa application process begin. After standing again in the long line at Window B, everything had to be verified. After that, we moved to another line leading to the even smaller Window A. Another morning was thus wasted. Window A finally gave us our visas.

I showed my woman friend the same sites I had visited alone nine years earlier. The sites were wonderful, but Nepal had become much more touristed by my fellow backpackers. There were also too many trucks on the roads around Kathmandu, making bicycle riding too dangerous. We stayed in the area around central Durbar Square, the main tourist zone, appropriately nicknamed Freak Street. That was where most of the choices were for eating and staying.

I followed the guidebook's walking tours around the city. They were well worth it. The guesthouse had very unreliable hot water. So, between cold showers, wide swings in temperature, and the billowing clouds of dust, we both caught colds. Despite it being the dry season with normally zero milligrams of rain, it poured rain for two days straight.

We took the 'mail' bus to Lumbini (birthplace of Buddha) on the Indian border. The trip took eight hours rather than the normal ten. Unfortunately, my seat was right above the rear wheel, which rattled my bones the whole way. With cold, wet feet, my nearly gone cold returned. Another reminder: on long bus rides, always try to sit in the front, behind the driver, for the smoothest ride.

We spent the night in Lumbini before entering India the following day. It was hard to sleep between the swarms of mosquitoes and the snoring neighbor in the room beside ours. We did not use the cold shower that was available. Fortunately, we managed to get some sleep and were ready for the travails of traveling in India by early the next morning.

Women Breaking Rocks under the Hot Hot Sun

India 1995

Creative Sex on the Temple Walls

I resigned from Thai Leader in the autumn of 1995 because I needed a change. I decided to do more traveling in the region before returning to the US. When I first visited India in 1987, I divided the country into two parts and concentrated on one of them, saving the other part for a later trip. I had done the same for China in the 1980's, but I divided it into three parts. It was now time to visit the second half.

For this trip, I chose winter to visit, the best season in terms of climate. Before visiting the south, the area of the country I reserved for my second visit, I had to fill a major gap in the north, the capital city of New Delhi. Travel in India is done mostly by train. This trip was not unusual. The fourteen-hour trip took over twenty hours.

Though most have heard the name 'New Delhi', there is also an Old Delhi, which was the capital of the Moghul empire. It is similar to any other old city in India with its narrow streets and crowded chaos, with its vibrant markets and historic charm. There one can see the grand Jama Masjid Mosque and the Red Fort, the residence of the Moghul emperors, and the nearby Chandi Chowk, a large sprawling market selling all things Indian.

New Delhi, on the other hand, was the capital during the British era. Today it is the home of India's modern government and bureaucracy. It is nicely laid out with large, leafy, tree-lined, quiet streets where armies of gardeners and others work on the grounds of the mansions from a bygone era. It almost made one want to be a part of the ruling class, as a cog in the machine of the British Raj back when the sun never set on the British Empire. Each of these two by itself would be a huge city. Together, they have a combined population of over sixteen million.

A day trip south is the impressive UNESCO designated Qutab Minar complex. Construction started in 1199 to celebrate the Muslim victory over the last of the Hindu rulers. Each succeeding sultan added more to the tower until it reached its last and tallest stage in 1368. The mosque was also built in 1199 from the demolished ruins of twenty-seven Jain and Hindu temples, according to the inscription at the entrance. Inside the grounds of the fallen mosque stands the famous seven meter/twenty-three foot high Iron Pillar, which remains incredibly rust-free to this day. It was built sometime around 400 AD.

Surrounding the city are many ruins of various palaces, tombs, forts, etc. all crumbling into the hot, dusty earth. They were equally grand, if not more so, but by not being in a guidebook, they were empty of tourists. This made them very pleasant to visit.

The National Museum heavily emphasized Hindu statuary with some Buddhist, too. It even had Mayan, Aztec, Inca, and examples from the indigenous peoples of the northwest US. What was glaringly absent was anything from the long Muslim period. The country needs to rethink its heritage and past.

The Crafts Museum was the highlight of all the indoor attractions. India is exceedingly rich in its arts and crafts. The textile section was particularly impressive. The best part for me was a village of houses and buildings representing the architecture from all the national regions in an open-air space. One could wander all afternoon among the structures. It was obvious to me that the National Museum was arranged and managed by bureaucrats. Whereas the Crafts Museum was a labor of love. It was clear even from the inscriptions.

To break up the trip south, we stopped and visited Gwalior, 300 kilometers/200 miles from Delhi. Located in the State of Madhya Pradesh, a branch of the Huns built their capital here in the 5th century AD. As with the rest of the country, it passed through many empires and dynasties until it became part of modern India.

I had a truly incredible experience there. We had to take a motorized rickshaw somewhere. When I bargained over the price, the driver insisted he use the meter. Wow, what a concept!

Stopping at Jhansi in eastern Madhya Pradesh, we took a bus another eighteen kilometers/eleven miles to Orchha, where we stayed in a wing of the Jehangir Mahal Palace. From the palace walls, we had magnificent views in all directions. There is not much to the current village, but within it, surrounding it, and as far as the eye could see were ruins of what was once a major capital city. Very often on my travels I find such places. My reaction is always, 'My, how the mighty have fallen!' It was the highlight of my trip so far.

Returning to Jhansi, we took a six-hour, very crowded bus ride to Khajuraho, 175 kilometers/110 miles away. That makes the average speed of an inter-city bus to be less than thirty kilometers/twenty miles an hour. On the bright side, the entire exterior of the bus was decked out in flowers, like a Taiwanese hearse.

Khajuraho is somewhat north of the geographic center of India. Its fame rests on the beautiful temple complex. The outer rock walls of the Hindu and Jain temples are covered in erotic carvings. The imagination of positions and the number of partners is comparable to the Kama Sutra. They were built between 880 and 1000 AD.

The temple complex was forgotten and hidden by undergrowth until British travelers discovered it in 1838. Since this was only one year after Victoria ascended the throne, perhaps the minds of the Brits were not yet polluted by what would be known as Victorian 'morality'.

My grandmother had an old spinster friend living with her as a friend and confident but often served as a maid or lady-in-waiting. She was cut whole from the prudish cloth of this pseudo morality. She made sure that all the sofa and chair legs were covered in a wraparound cloth so as not to arouse us menfolk. The picnic table in the backyard escaped her silly concerns, probably because its legs were modestly crossed.

We visited the various temples by bicycle. Since the electricity was out across town, I had to keep farmers' hours, basing my day on the availability of sunlight. Fortunately, village life used little electricity. Wood stoves and kerosene lamps dampened the effect nicely.

The next day we returned to Jhansi by bus, this time arriving an hour early. From there, I took the Punjab Mail Express train to Sanchi for the five-hour trip. The 'Express' arrived an hour late. Sanchi is famous for its large complex of Buddhist stupas, monasteries, and temples built by Emperor Ashoka and others, starting from 300 BC. The great stupa is one of the oldest stone structures in India.

The historical Buddha, known as Gautama and Siddhartha, lived around the year 500 BC. For the first four hundred years of the religion, he was never depicted as human. Various symbols were used instead, including dharma wheels, an empty throne, the Bodhi tree, where he achieved liberation after long meditation, etc. Such is the case with the earliest temples at Sanchi.

Interestingly, there were no Buddhist texts until four hundred years after the great man lived. No one really knows what the Buddha said or thought. In contrast, the earliest account of the life of Jesus is the Gospel of Mark, written about forty-five years after the crucifixion. Still, it is enough time for memories to fade or be distorted.

When we visited, pilgrims from Sri Lanka inundated the town. It was hard to find a hotel room. I ended up sharing a single bed with my girlfriend, a bed too small for one person. But we were young and did not mind the intimacy.

Bhopal, the capital of the state of Madhya Pradesh, is less than a two-hour train ride from Sanchi. I visited the local British Council, one of the many UK government-funded cultural centers found around the world. I used them mainly to spend a few hours drying off my sweaty body in the air-conditioned library, reading The Economist and the like to catch up on world news.

This one had an exhibition of old photos of Bhopal from 150 years earlier. Except for the chaotic electric and phone lines hanging all around, the streets outside looked the same as the photos on the walls. We did a day trip to the south of the city to see the prehistoric cave paintings from 100,000 years ago. The red painted hunting scenes are very similar to others around the world, showing how similar life was for all early humans.

Bhopal was also the site of the terrible industrial accident at the Union Carbide pesticide factory in 1984. Half a million people were exposed to highly toxic chemicals leaked into the air, resulting in the deaths of nearly 18,000 people. Eventually, it was determined that the criminal negligence and incompetence of the local Indian factory management caused the disaster.

Making my way to Bombay, we stopped at Indore, Dhar, and Mandu, the ruined site of an ancient capital city. The trip was arduous, mostly because of the long, unpleasant bus journeys. I also suffered from commonly occurring stomach problems and colds throughout my travels in India. This was due to the general unsanitary water, food, and environment, exasperated by the generally difficult conditions of long-distance overland travel. Fortunately, because of my excellent youthful constitution and natural energy, I persevered.

I used to smoke when I lived in Thailand (Lucky Strikes or Camels). I always preferred the tactile experience of using matches. After traveling through Maharashtra State for only a brief time, I noticed the signs were written in the same script as Thai. I happened to have a Thai matchbox with me. I showed it to the locals. Yes, it was the same script, but they could make no sense of it. They could pronounce the letters in their language. That was the extent of it. It was the same as Westerners trying to make sense of Vietnamese, which uses the Latin alphabet.

This is not surprising when one understands the history of Southeast Asia. India spread its religions and written languages throughout the region. When the great emperor, Ashoka, conquered most of the Indian subcontinent two thousand two hundred years ago, he sent Buddhist missionaries with their various written languages to places like Burma, Thailand, Cambodia, and Indonesia. that had none of their own scripts at the time. Later, India continued its influence through Hinduism and trade. One can see evidence of this in the great ancient Buddhist monuments and palace art across the region. Many foreign travelers are familiar with the wonderful, casteless Hinduism of Bali.

The Wheel of Life

India 1995

The Followers of Saint Thomas

After arriving in the surprisingly clean and pleasant city of Bombay, I perked up. If I had to live in India, this would be the place. The center was full of grand British colonial architecture and wide plazas. I visited the primary tourist sites of museums and the like. A highlight was the UNESCO Elephanta Caves on an island eleven kilometers/eight miles by boat from the jetty by the famous Gate of India. The island's caves, named because of the elephant statues, are impressive with their three-headed Siva and other Hindu and Buddhist rock carvings from 500 AD.

Much of the city consists of dilapidated slums, as in every Indian city. They were once middle-class neighborhoods, but after decades of rent control, they deteriorated to their current state. After years of constantly increasing prices, landlords could not afford to repair and renovate their properties, paying 1995 prices while receiving 1965 rent.

We stayed in a hotel outside the city center. We took a local commuter train into the center. The train was so crowded that I did what hundreds of other passengers did and sat on the roof. We had to duck low when we passed under an overpass. Shanty shacks were built alongside the tracks as close as they could without a passing train hitting them. Imagine a town of poverty with a railroad as the center street.

Money is a serious problem in the world's poorer countries. Coins are more expensive to stamp than printing small, cheap quality notes. The smaller denominations change hands very often and become worn out quickly. These small change bills are kept in circulation way past their time. So, they become rather tatty, sometimes even missing a part that has fallen off. One must be careful not to accept notes as change that are in an advanced state of tattiness, as it may be difficult to have someone else accept them later. This causes a general shortage of money in circulation. May the money gods help you if you try to get change for a high denomination bill anywhere, including the banks.

Once I boarded a public bus in Bombay, where the driver refused to accept my gently used, only somewhat tatty note. Weary of this game, I ignored him and sat down. He continued driving his route for a while until he stopped to call a policeman to board and fine me for not paying my fare. I explained to him that I had offered to pay and showed him the note. He had to admit that it was useable within the context of India, but he had to take the side of the bus driver. Rather than fine me, he just threw me off the bus.

When the next bus arrived. I entered and gave the driver the very same note as the other one who had made such a fuss over it. He accepted it without question. This experience highlights two things. One is the general problem of using small notes in such countries. The other is that a foreign traveler finds pettiness more often than in more developed countries. The first driver was being petty in such a way. A wonderful Chinese expression captures it perfectly. He was trying to find bones in an egg (雞蛋裡挑骨頭).

An enormous problem nationwide, homelessness is a particularly severe problem in Bombay. At night they come out and claim their special spot, spreading their mats on the sidewalk. The better sleeping spots are passed down from generation to generation. Everyone knows who 'owns' what, thereby avoiding potentially violent conflicts.

I treated us to a stay at a nearby resort on the Indian Ocean. Being off season, we could stay in a private cabin with three meals a day for a very reasonable price. But we had to get there first. That required a local train, followed by a local bus, then a ferry, and finally a horse cart to the Catholic fishing village neighboring the resort.

It was a fine rest after the tribulations of traveling in India. There were no other guests but us. The food was plentiful and excellent. The service was unusually good for the sub-continent. It rained often, and the wind blew down many palm fronds from the trees. I continued my tradition of swimming in all the seas of the world. This one being the Indian Ocean, or the Arabian Sea, or, as I decided, both.

A three-hour train ride south brought me to the lush hill station of Lonavala, where the wonderful Karla and Bhaja Caves are located. These ancient Buddhist shrines were carved out of the rock about two thousand years ago. There was an ugly, garish pink Hindu temple built in front of the entrance. It caused me to wonder why anyone would give up the blissful serenity of casteless Buddhism to become a Hindu again.

Lonavala is clearly a weekend getaway for Indians from Bombay and Pune. The town was geared toward them. In the plaza outside my hotel window at night, there was a traditional wedding celebration. Such things must be seen to be believed. They are quite a spectacle with their colorfully painted elephants, joyful traditional music, gaily dressed crowds with thousands of flowers decked out in a multitude of ways. It lasted until the wee hours, but I did not mind. The event was worth it.

Arriving in Bijapur in Karnataka State required us to leap onto the last car of a moving train leaving the station. Sitting on wooden slat benches for ten and a half hours was grueling. We sat in the middle of fields for one and a half hours for no obvious reason. Was it going too fast for the schedule? Not likely. It must have been for another unfathomable reason.

Bijapur is famous for the incredibly huge but tasteful mausoleum of Ibrahim Adil Shah II, the sultan of the Bijapur Sultanate from 1580 to 1627. The mausoleum was completed in 1626, just in time for its benefactor to move in. As with all the great kings of ancient times, the first thing they did when they ascended the throne was to start construction on their huge and overwhelming tomb. The decades it took to construct it meant that, with proper planning and a lot of luck, the tomb might be completed before the king needed to use it. Often, they were completed years after the king had already expired. His filial son would hopefully respect his father's last wishes.

To enter the tomb, we had to take off our shoes in respect to the dead king. I climbed up the tower to the base of the dome. There I experienced something from Dante's Inferno. Indian tourists were running around the base shrieking like banshees. The wonderful acoustics of the dome echoed each one a dozen times. The offensive din forced us back down and out. Passing the blood red betelnut-stained walls of the stairway did not increase my respect for the local tourists.

Traveling to Badami required a six-hour bus ride. The electricity went out right before dinnertime. The only places we found serving dinner were the arak drinking holes around the station. We ordered vegetable fried rice and received instead one packet worth of instant soup noodles, fried for the two of us. I had to laugh. Traveling requires a keen sense of humor.

The small town of Badami was once the capital of the Chalukya kingdom that dominated the region 1500 years ago, but now is just a pale remnant of its impressive past. Around the town are many caves carved before 500 AD, dedicated to Vishnu, Shiva, Jain, and

Buddhist deities. There were also early examples of Hindu temple architecture.

Passing through Hospet, we arrived in Hampi by mid-afternoon. We stayed at a place where we had to use the public toilets and showers across the street. Fortunately, they were quite clean. All the locals were creative in finding ways to extract money from tourists. Anyone who had an extra room opened a guest house or a restaurant.

Hampi was once the capital of the Hindu Vijayanagar Empire, one of the most important in Indian history. It ruled most of southern India from 1336 to 1565. After it lost an important battle to the Muslim Deccan Sultanates in 1565, its capital at Hampi was systematically pillaged and destroyed over six months. Though it managed to continue until 1646, it was just a rump of what it once was.

Portuguese travelers from Goa wrote extensively about the grandeur they found there. In 1500, it was the second largest city in the world after Beijing, with a population of over half a million. The over 1,600 ruins spread all over this UNESCO site attest to that. When we visited it, the population was eight hundred.

The night we were there, the locals held a large celebration of the full moon. The Hindu devotees of the large, shining, nocturnal orb paraded images of Shiva and his nicely curved consort, Parvati, through the ruins with much beating of drums. As is normal with the emotional people of India, the celebration was most fervent, even feverish. They even had a boy possessed by something. We attended a backpacker's party by the river, partaking of the noble herb, enjoying the moon's reflections and luminations in a much calmer way.

We took the afternoon bus back to Hospet, the main city near Hampi, to spend the night. The following day we took the train to Bangalore, probably the most modern city in India with its hundreds of call centers for large US and European companies. It is a center of India's high-tech industry. We left our backpacks at the train station and explored the city for the day, including buying our plane tickets from Calcutta back to Bangkok.

Mysore was our next stop on our trip south. We arrived there in the early evening. The following day we took a bus to see the impressive 12th century Sri Chamundeshwari Temple. Our bus broke down before we could leave the station. The second bus had to be jump started. All of this was normal, except that on the same day India sent a rocket into space to place a satellite in orbit.

An example of the books I read then is Kafka's The Castle. It was ironic in that India may be the most bureaucratic country in the world. Being stuck in a Kafkian bureaucratic nightmare anywhere would be terrible, but I imagine in India it would be akin to being in one of the middle rings of Dante's Inferno.

I also finished A Second Treasury of Kahlil Gibran, a collection of short stories by the author of The Prophet, his most famous book. As with everything he wrote, his stories are full of inspiring tales of Love and Beauty. I eventually read everything he wrote, loving every poetic line.

The next stop was Hassan, still in Karnataka State. This city is in the middle of a dozen or more wonderful Jain and Hindu (Vishnu) temples built nearly 900 years ago. They were similar in design. Quite amusing rock carvings covered the exterior walls. I had to smile when I saw a stone carved woman orally pleasuring a stone man in front of her while another was taking her from behind. There was no esoteric metaphor explanation possible. It was just straight up good times being had by all. I consider it a wonderful celebration of life.

We stayed in a hotel for middle class Indian tourists. It was air-conditioned with equipment from the 1950's when such things first appeared. It would have been better with a common ceiling fan, a mosquito net, and open windows. The windowless bathrooms, where the air conditioning did not reach, had a small open space between the wall and the ceiling to allow air to flow between them. The space was enough for someone to peek over if they were standing on something.

While I was taking a shower, I noticed that the husband of the middle-aged couple staying next door was looking over this space at me. When he realized I saw him, he immediately jumped down from whatever he was standing on. No doubt, he was hoping to see my Taiwanese girlfriend in the shower, or was he?

After weeks in the interior, we returned to the sea at Mangalore, on the very southwest corner of Karnataka State. Next, we arrived in Calicut in Kerela State. Calicut gave us the word 'calico' for the cloth it exported (and the cat). It was also where Vasco de Gama arrived in 1498, the first European navigator who sailed around Africa and stepped foot in India.

The first thing a foreigner notices in Kerala State is the well-mannered and educated people there. They understand the purpose of lines and behave generally well on all occasions. Even more importantly, the population is evenly divided between Hindus, Muslims, and Christians (Syrian Coptic Orthodox from the time when Saint Thomas lived in India as a missionary). All three groups live in harmony, respecting each other's practices and beliefs. One notices this even in the food of the restaurants, including excellent beef curries in the Christian eateries. There was none of the sectarian violence so common elsewhere in India.

Much later, when email existed, I had once asked my sea captain brother where his ship was. He was delivering supplies to the military base in Diego Garcia, a British possession in the middle of the Indian Ocean. He could not tell me where he was due to military secrecy. But he gave me a hint. He was sailing past where Saint Thomas had lived and proselytized. I knew exactly where he was.

We visited a predominately Christian town, where all the inhabitants were worshiping in church. Their beliefs appeared similar to the Egyptian Coptics, including men and women sitting on separate sides of the church. It is incredible to think that a large group of isolated Christians could thrive for nearly two thousand years. They were direct descendants of the first converts of one of the Apostles. He, like me, was the doubting one.

Joyful Villagers

India 1996

Hare Krishna

We continued down the coast to Cochin. We saw a performance of the incredible Kathakali dance, a traditional dance that started 500 years ago. To me, it is one of the most incredible examples of traditional dance anywhere, except perhaps classical Western ballet.

The dancers are men who have trained since they were young boys. They use elaborate, colorful make-up and costumes. The dancers use dramatic facial expressions, stylized gestures, and body movements. The performance combines elements of dance, theater, music, and mime to present tales from Hindu epics like the Ramayana and the Mahabharata. Their complex makeup transforms the only male dancers into characters from mythology, with assorted colors representing gods, heroes, or demons.

The performance we saw was the story of Prince Jaina and the maiden demoness. It started with the two men dancers putting on their makeup on stage, explaining the significance of the various vibrant colors. A green face with vibrant red lips and a white beard represents a divine noble character such as Prince Jaina. Red faces represent demons, and yellow is the color of women and sages. The make-up is made from natural pigments in coconut oil or sometimes sandalwood mixed in water.

After the two had put on their makeup, they exercised their faces for the required expressions of the dance. It was amazing to watch their eyes spin around and their eyebrows leap up and down. The impressive costumes were another source of wonder. They made the dancers appear quite large. The maiden demoness had particularly large thighs and hips to accentuate this womanly characteristic. Then they explained the many varied gestures.

Several percussionists and a singer (in Sanskrit) provided the music. The dancers say nothing throughout the performance, relying on gestures and movements to tell the story. The stories normally come from the ancient Hindu classics of the Ramayana, the Mahabharata, and the Bhagavata Purana.

In this performance, the story unfolds with Prince Jaina, a noble denizen in a heaven-like place, meeting a beautiful maiden. She is smitten with him and tries to entice him to run away with her and marry her. He agrees but tells her that he must first gain his father's permission. Her passion rises to a crescendo, telling him she cannot live without him. She must have him now!

He starts to suspect that she is not really a heavenly being, as they are much more decorous and reserved. Realizing she has failed in her craftiness, she reverts to her original demoness self and attacks him. He prevails, cuts off her ears, nose, and breasts (!), then drives her from the heavenly sphere. Interestingly, I had seen that very story painted on a wall of a palace I had visited that same morning. This unforgettable performance thoroughly impressed me. UNESCO is completely correct in naming Kathakali dance a Masterpiece of the Oral and Intangible Heritage of Humanity.

My love for Kerala, my favorite state of India, did not end there. The next day we took a boat trip through the inland waterway to Kollam, eight hours away. I enjoyed every minute. The boat passed small fishing villages with their nets drying on wooden frames. Great shady trees with their canopy above protected us from the strong southern sun the whole way. Various monkeys and tropical birds flitted about above us. We passed a thousand-year-old Buddhist stupa and a place where a famous poet drowned.

We stopped for lunch at a small hamlet, where we had a traditional Kerala thali plate served on a large banana leaf. Unlike most curries in the south of India, this one was pleasantly mild. Later we stopped for a tea break at another, larger town. We had to pass through one set of very rusty locks, though the water level was only about ten centimeters/four inches different between the two sides. We stopped at an ashram run by a female guru. I did not know such beings existed. Several middle-aged women got on and off at that stop.

After we arrived in Kollam, there was a big rush to the train station. We tried to get sleeper berths to Madurai in Tamil Nadu. They were not available, and so we spent the night at the appropriately named Rail View Hotel across from the station. The first thing I did the next morning was to go to the station and get sleeper tickets for that night's train to Madurai. After that, we walked around town and dipped our feet into the waters of the Indian Ocean at the nearby beach.

We arrived early in the morning. After checking into a simple hotel, we walked to the overwhelming Shree Meenakshi Amman Temple. The temple's fourteen gaudily colorful gopurams (gateway towers) dominated the city skyline. Covered in bright carvings of Hindu gods, the Dravidian-style temple is a major pilgrimage site for many millions of Indians every year.

I stood in the lengthy line to enter. When I approached the entrance, temple guards with long stout sticks threatened to beat me if I tried to enter. Neither Untouchables nor foreigners were allowed in. So much for the universal appeal of Hinduism.

One of the main things to do in Madurai is to have clothes made at the hundreds of tailor stalls. The trick is to buy the cloth from any of the many cloth sellers somewhere else and then find a tailor to make the clothes. Otherwise, tourists pay only ten rupees for the tailoring but remarkably unreasonable prices for the cloth at the same tailor's shop.

The next day we visited the ruins of the Thirumalai Nayakkar Palace, within walking distance of the temple. There was not much left of the palace, but the ruined dance hall made it worthwhile. Both the temple and palace were built in the 1600's by the Nayak Dynasty (1565 to 1781).

We continued our journey through Tamil Nadu and visited Tiruchirappalli. The express train had no assigned seats. So, despite being third in line when the door opened, we just barely managed to find seats, and this was even with me fighting to get on like the best of them. There were men dressed in red who were most aggressive in finding seats. They would grab four each and then sell them for ten rupees per space. It is one way to make a living, I guess.

We spent the rest of the day washing clothes and buying train tickets out of there. We took a city bus to the Jambukeswarar Akilandeswari Temple, dedicated to Shiva. Untouchables and foreigners were not allowed to enter. A temple tout hassled us the whole time we wandered the grounds outside. Though I could not see the mighty lingam (a waist-high stone pillar, representing Shiva's phallic shlong), I could appreciate the yonis (flowers representing quims, the female sex organ) on the tiles of the grounds. Sri Ranganathaswamy Temple, with intricately carved gopurams dedicated to Vishnu, was as uptight about Untouchables and foreigners as the Shiva temple was. May the gods forbid that our polluting shadows touch the erect sacred stone shafts!

It seems to me that Hinduism started as several different religions with many gods and their incarnations, which ended up under the overarching canopy of Hinduism. Indians are wonderfully comfortable worshiping all of them. This makes sense if one considers that they are all representations of the same Divine Spirit.

Christians, Muslims, Jews, and other monotheist religions do not understand this. But then neither do the Hindus, as evidenced by their violence against the Muslims living in their midst.

The next city we visited in Tamil Nadu was Thanjavur. Its many temples include the 11th century Brihadeeswarar Temple, a vast Chola dynasty–era (8th to the 13th centuries) complex with a frescoed interior. The Thanjavur Maratha Palace is home to the centuries-old Saraswathi Mahal Library, with palm-leaf manuscripts and old Chinese prints of imaginative ways to torture, and the Thanjavur Art Gallery, with bronze and stone religious statues.

A forty-five-minute bus ride from the insanely chaotic station took us to Mahabalipuram on the Bay of Bengal. The city was overwhelmed with Indian tourists. It is also full of the rap-tap-tapping of stone carvers. The Vishnu temple by the sea was in a fantastic location. We sanctified ourselves in the waters of the Bay of Bengal.

Most of our meals were thali plates, usually for around ten rupees. The thali plate itself is made of aluminum with indented sections to hold various foods the servers place in them. They reminded me of frozen TV dinners, but not the food. The food was various curries, usually vegetarian, with dahl (lentil) soup and rotis (chapatis) or rice.

Restaurants usually charged more for takeout with their 'package charge', not unlike Western companies charging more for buying concert tickets online with their 'convenience' fees. Both are absurd and make no sense.

I have mentioned various examples of corruption in my travel accounts. One memorable example leaps to mind. India is a country with many languages that uses English so the various peoples can communicate with each other. Many touts, beggars, kiosk owners, and generally less established people come from elsewhere, sometimes from the other end of the country.

In a certain unnamed city, by chance I came across two policemen beating a man in the street. Apparently, he was caught pick-pocketing a man who was standing nearby. The would-be thief was crying out to the incensed victim, "Please, sir, tell them you only had two hundred rupees, not five hundred". The police were demanding the thief to hand over the higher sum to share the difference with each other. But the unlucky thief did not have any more money. That probably explained why he was trying to steal it in the first place.

We continued up the coast by train to Madras. I extended our plane reservations to Bangkok. I also arranged our train tickets with sleeping berths to Puri, which would take twenty-four hours. We had to be well rested and prepared, starting with a good night's sleep in a hotel bed and buying provisions to eat for the entire journey.

We saw all the major sights of one of India's most important cities. During the day, we passed through a section of the city filled with bookshops. There was also a book fair nearby. I bought a copy of the Bhagavad Gita. This ranks as one of the outstanding books of world literature. Many Westerners of a certain age may remember the Hare Krishnas wearing their robes while joyfully dancing and chanting Hara Krishna on street corners. They were considered a strange cult to be distrusted.

They are, in fact, members of the largest Hindu religious group. They are followers of Krishna, a very approachable, playful incarnation of Vishnu, usually depicted as a blue skinned young man with his eyes on the sweet milkmaids bathing nude in the river. He is a likeable rogue.

One often met these Hare Krishnas at Western airports and bus stations, handing out copies of the Bhagavad Gita. If one had any understanding of Indian culture and Hinduism, one should have gladly accepted it and read it with great interest. I read the copy one of them gave me at an airport and the copy I bought in Madras. I have read the scriptures of all the major religions of the world, including the Bible from cover to cover (like a novel), the Koran twice, multitudes of Buddhist writings, various Jewish texts, etc.

The Bhagavad (Holy) Gita was written over 2000 years ago. It is without question the most important pan-Hindu scripture. It represents Hinduism at its best. To me, rather than a religious text, it contains a philosophy that actually makes sense, an understanding of how the human mind works that would make any modern psychologist blush. It describes a healthy way of living and a mindset that is very appropriate for anyone trying to live in this modern age. I could write a whole lecture about this astounding book, but I will end by encouraging my readers to read it themselves.

Farmer's Cart

India 1995

Chasing the Dragon

And Opium for Breakfast

We continued up the east coast to Puri, a fishing village on the Karella coast. I visited there in 1985 and enjoyed it immensely. We took a rickshaw to the Z Hotel, where I stayed on my first visit. I could not believe we could fit ourselves and everything else into the rickshaw meant for one person. We arrived around midnight. The hotel manager said that they were full. So, I left my girlfriend and our luggage there while I went searching for a place to stay.

Everything was full due to tourists from Calcutta. It was the day before New Year's Eve. I returned two hours later without finding any vacant room. I considered sleeping on the beach. But as I returned, the owner, who lived in the guesthouse, also arrived. I asked him if we could sleep on the sofa in the lobby until the next morning, like I had done the first time I stayed there.

He did not think that was a good idea until I reminded him that we had chased the dragon (snorting heroin that was cut with the gods know what) together when I stayed there in 1987. It worked like a secret code. Remembering me, he smiled and agreed with my suggestion. He invited us to have vegetable curry with him for a very late dinner.

We had to get up at 0700 the next morning when they opened. After waiting until 0900, the check-out time, we were rewarded with a single room for me and a place in the women's dorm for her.

Everything worked out well. We had had little sleep for a few nights, but we were young and could bounce back quickly.

The small, peaceful fishing village that I remembered had changed for the worse. Half the village was filled with thirty ugly concrete guesthouses that were not there eight years earlier. The Government Ganja Shops (printed in large letters in English above the little kiosk) in the main town were no longer in conspicuous places like before but were hidden down alleys, probably to discourage the ever-growing number of foreign tourists from finding them. I found one the next day anyway.

As was the case eight years before, in the line with me were day laborers, rickshaw drivers, construction workers, etc. Bang was replaced by the better known ganja for smoking. I bought one and a half tolas (eighteen grams) of the best quality ganja for fifty rupees (a little less than one US dollars). The second quality cost forty rupees. I also bought half a tola of opium for seventy-five rupees. For my non-metric readers, there are twenty-eight grams in an ounce and twelve grams in a tola.

Without paper or a pipe, I had to be creative. I bought a pack of filterless cigarettes for four rupees! To me, a pack of cigarettes for about seven cents is practically free. Even so, smoking was considered an unaffordable luxury for most. It was normal for kiosks to sell individual cigarettes. I replaced the tobacco with ganja, problem solved. I made little balls from the black, sticky opium and simply swallowed them (no chewing!) like the traditional Chinese medicine it is.

On the second night, the owner invited me to chase the dragon with him again. He had not changed in the intervening eight years. The next morning, I regretted it, probably more from whatever it was cut with than the heroin itself. Heroin (and cocaine) is usually cut (mixed with other cheaper ingredients) to lower the cost to the seller.

Typical cutting ingredients can include any white powder, like baking soda, laundry detergent, starch, talcum powder, etc. Users never know what they are getting, nor the purity of the desired ingredient. That was the last time I did anything that was a white powder. As the US government anti-drug warnings on television in the 1960's and 1970's put it: "Why do you think they call it 'dope', dope?"

Later that evening, the hotel owner, his girlfriend, and a few other Indian friends visited me in my room to partake of my noble herb. I did not mind, as I had bought too much anyway. His girlfriend rewarded me with a pack of rolling papers. So, I could roll my joints the traditional American way.

I spent a day in nearby Bhubaneswar trying to buy our tickets with sleeping berths to Calcutta, our final destination in India. The two-hour bus ride each way was not enough. I returned empty-handed.

I spent the entire next day trying to do the same. Over eight hours later at the chaotic station, with various unhelpful employees providing me with much incorrect information, I still was unsuccessful. That was almost the same amount of time that the trip would take to Calcutta. The next day we checked out and tried again. We were unsuccessful once more and had to spend a night at a rundown hotel near the station. We were able to get sleeping berths for the following night. I had originally planned to visit Puri for two days. We were there for five.

On the bright side, I was able to show her the magnificent stone Sun Chariot temple at Konarak. Built 800 years ago with no Hindu figures, it made me think it was dedicated to a sun god religion that was later subsumed into Hinduism. We also visited the Jagannath Temple, the most famous temple in Puri. This is another example of an originally non-Hindu religion later absorbed by the overwhelming Hinduism, in this case as one of the many incarnations of Vishnu. The worship procedures, sacraments, and rituals associated with Jagannath are syncretic and include rites that are uncommon in Hinduism.

The three gods are Jagannath, his brother, and sister. Their idols are bizarre, like exaggerated cartoon characters (meant with no disrespect). The idols of these three gods are carved and decorated wooden stumps with large round eyes and colorful faces. They have no hands or legs. But how are they any different from Shiva's mighty stone phallic shaft that is the center of every temple dedicated to him?

Once a year during the Rath Yatra festival, they are placed on huge wooden chariots two or three stories tall. Hundreds of fanatical devotees push and pull these chariots through the mobbed city streets. Others, even more gripped by insane devotion, throw themselves under the heavy chariot wheels as they pass. The English word 'juggernaut' comes from the word 'Jagannath'. It must have greatly impressed the Brits when they first saw it centuries ago.

We arrived in Calcutta, our last stop before returning to Thailand. We had both been there eight years earlier. The main thing that was new was the metro system, which worked well. We refunded our Air India tickets for significantly cheaper ones on Druk Air. I was surprised at how easy the refund process was. Though it was within the rules, I was expecting a major hassle.

As with every Indian city we visited, I had to spend a few hours finding a place to stay. In the days before the internet and cell phones, there was no way to contact a hotel to make reservations. Even calling from a payphone was impossible in most of the developing world. Even if they existed, they probably did not work. We ended up staying at the Salvation Army Hostel in a room with a bath for 120 rupees (slightly more than two US dollars).

Sadhus are a common sight in India. They are Hindu holy men who sleep wherever and eat whatever they can. The local people support them, so they are not beggars. They let their hair and beards grow with no interest in haircare or appearance (good for them!). Their demeanor is dignified. They are men who have decided to leave all social life and pursue a spiritual journey.

What fascinates me is the tradition of men going through the four stages of life: childhood and studies, career and family man, retired grandfather, and finally a renounced life – the life of a sadhu. Many sadhus had successful careers with large, contented families in their past. One cannot judge them as common beggars. They are wandering holy men, ascetic mendicants who help consume the bad karma of society.

They travel on foot as pilgrims to the multitude of holy sites throughout the country. Wearing simple robes or even little or nothing at all, their days are filled with meditation, yoga, chanting, prayer, etc. They have renounced all status, wealth, and family ties. I just find that a wonderful way to spend the last years of life.

As for us, we filled our last few days there by wandering through markets and enjoying the personality of the city. We had traveled a great distance around India. After three months, it was time to leave. I shaved my three-month-old wild sadhu-like beard at a street barber and prepared for what lay in store in Thailand. It was an incredible journey filled with memories to last a lifetime.

Making Cotton Thread by Hand

1996

Indochina

Cambodia 1996

Giant Stone Heads

Lurking in the Forest

I returned to Bangkok for two weeks in January 1996 after traveling in India for three months. My Corsican friend let us stay in the small apartment above a convenience store they owned in Wattakei, a suburb of Bangkok, about two hours by public transport. We spent a night at the beautiful house full of Thai antiques of another French friend and his Taiwanese wife. They were always living from hand to mouth. I tried to use their phone, but it did not work because they had not paid the telephone bill. We visited various other friends before flying to Phnom Penh, the capital of Cambodia.

Phnom Penh was a sprawling city of 700,000. No building was taller than five floors. The traffic was noticeably light, mainly consisting of motorbikes, bicycles, and bicycle rickshaws, where the passenger sits in front of the driver rather than behind him as in India. There were many ethnic Chinese there, so eating was not a problem. It was easy to find excellent baguettes that would have made most any boulangerie in Paris proud. Clearly, they were a gift from their French colonizers.

The French influence continues. There was an enormous, newly built building surrounded by a park and wrought iron fences that would have felt comfortable on a leafy boulevard in one of the double-digit arrondissements in Paris. It was the home of Phnom Penh's Alliance Français, France's mission to promote French culture and language around the world. I attended French language classes in ones located in Hong Kong and Chicago. A young

Frenchman could choose to work in one of these rather than do military service. That would have been my choice, too.

The curious thing was that despite the French government's serious and costly attempt to promote their wonderful language and culture to their ex-colony; it simply did not meet the interests of the locals. Very few of them attended classes there. Nearby was a rat warren of alleys with many dozens of one room holes in the wall of private English language schools filled with hundreds of Cambodians, young and not so young, learning English. I kind of felt bad for the French, but the market had spoken (oh, that is so Anglo-American!).

A quirky thing about Cambodia at the time was its use of both US dollars and the national currency of riels. For lower transactions, often both single dollars and riel notes were used together. They used only US dollars for higher value transactions. We walked everywhere, visiting the central market and the horrifying holocaust museum, documenting the terrors of the murderous Pol Pot years and his killing fields in the late 1970's.

Our next destination was Siem Reap upcountry, the home of many incredible temples covering a large, forested expanse. The most famous one is Angar Wat. We had to take a bus and then a boat trip across Tonlé Sap, the largest lake in Southeast Asia, to arrive there. The town was small, with about 10,000 people living there. The number of tourists there might have swelled the population by one percent. It was a small town changing from an agricultural center to a tourist one. It only had simple guesthouses and local restaurants. I understand now it is a small city with modern international resorts and a busy airport. I am glad I visited when I did.

The Khmer empire was founded in 802 as a Hindu kingdom centered in Siem Reap. So, the temples were mainly Hindu with some Buddhist. After the Thai Ayutthaya kingdom defeated them in 1351, the empire became its vassal state. After a failed uprising in 1431, the Thais sacked the city, and the population fled south, leaving the once great city in ruins to be reclaimed by dense forests. It was the largest city at the time with a probable population of one million.

Our guesthouse gave us a local map indicating where the temples were. Most importantly, it designated the safe area we could go, protected by Army patrols. Beyond the pale was Pol Pot's Khmer Rouge territory. These were the guerillas of the defeated Pol Pot regime after Vietnam invaded and threw them out of power. This fortuitous act ended one of the most murderous regimes in human history that massacred about twenty-five percent of its own people in the name of Marxist socialism.

I hired a motorcycle guide to take us around to visit the temples. Angar Wat, built in the early 1100's by King Suryavarman II, was the only temple that was reclaimed from the forest and renovated from its ruins. It sits in a cleared area on the other side of a large one hundred meter/yard lagoon. Sitting on the hill across the lagoon with the other backpackers, I reveled in its symmetrical beauty as the sunset bathed it in golden light. I was the only one there without a camera. I stopped bringing one because I noticed that people with cameras let the camera do the seeing. After seeing it with only my eyes, burning its image into my brain, I can remember it today like it was only yesterday.

As with almost every other temple besides Angar Wat, the forest was busy devouring the ruined temples. Fully grown trees occupied the central spaces of temples, with the large stones of the roof lying about on the exposed ground covered in moss. Monkeys and birds flitted about decayed and forgotten deities and demons. It was surreal to witness the slow process of Nature taking back what was once hers. It reminded me of when I was a child passing by an abandoned farm in Maine, where the already old trees had reclaimed the fields, the collapsed farmhouse, and the rotting barn.

As beautiful as Angar Wat is, it is not my favorite temple. That title falls to the Bayon Temple. It occupies the geographic center of the ancient city. It was one of the last state-built temples before the empire's collapse. What is most impressive are the 216 giant heads, each the height of a person standing, that peer down at us lowly supplicants from every angle and level of the temple. The serenely smiling faces are all identical, probably the face of the king, Jayavarman VII, who built the temple around 1300.

We returned to Phnom Penh by local transport, four hours in a jeepney. We were the only foreigners and sat in the back with everyone else with their sacks of fish and farm products. It seemed like every ten minutes we were stopped by an army checkpoint. Often, it was nothing more than a stick placed across the road. The teenagers in their ragged uniforms with flip-flops or even barefoot 'manned' them with their AK-47's. The cost to pass was about one US dollar and a pack or two of cigarettes that the driver paid. I thought at the time that Africa must be like this. They never hassled me, the lone non-Asian in the back. Once, however, one of the more professional roadblocks confiscated a sack full of still living turtles from one would-be smuggler. Dinner that night would be turtle soup for them.

The countryside reminded me of Thailand, with far fewer people. We passed a farming village where everyone was celebrating a local deity. There I saw one of the most incredible sights in all my travels. A group of men were dressed as demons in the best Asian tradition, with too long burial shroud sleeves and fiercely fanged masks. They walked on hidden stilts, making them tower over everyone at three meters/ten feet tall, swinging their arms dramatically with their sleeves flapping to the front and back. That was worth the entire trip, especially since it represented the living traditional culture of the countryside.

We returned to Phnom Penh for a few days before flying on to Saigon (now Ho Chi Minh City), the old capital of South Vietnam, a place that figured importantly during my early years in the 1960's. My journey through Cambodia was wonderful. The hordes of Chinese and other tourists had not discovered it yet, as they have now. It is another example of a place with its modern changes that I never want to return to and destroy the wonderful memories from a different time.

Country Life

Vietnam 1996

"The US Will Never Go to War Over Some Damn Dingdong"

President Roosevelt

The flight from Phnom Penh to Saigon was forty-five minutes long. I was back in a socialist country, yet some things never change. While going through immigration, the officer pushed a piece of paper across the counter to me with '$10' written on it while he was checking my passport and visa. I looked at it and laughed. He quickly took it back. I looked around at the other lines full of Asian travelers from various countries, who sheepishly paid the informal entry tax. The baggage handlers also stole the packs of cigarettes my girlfriend had in her luggage.

We stayed on the third floor of a guesthouse that required climbing two ladders. The climb was worth it as we had the whole large top floor to ourselves with windows and views on three sides. We were the only guests. The elderly woman living there treated us like family. We did not even have to hassle with police registration.

The first project was to work on our Lao visas. I visited the consulate to ask about the details which they gave me (cost, photos, validity, processing time, etc.). It took most of the morning. Later that day, I asked myself if the thirty-day validity was from when the visa was issued or from when we entered the country. Since I planned to travel much more in Vietnam, it was not a moot question.

I decided that rather than spend many mores hours to get that answer from the consulate, I could ask a travel agent who specializes in Laos.

The first one, despite her long explanation, obviously did not know. I went to another one. He did not know either. I suggested that if he were to call the consulate and find out, he could answer the next tourist who asked the same thing. He could not grasp that bit of free enterprise thinking and charged me for the call. It was valid from when entering the country. I returned to the consulate and applied for visas.

During those hours, I investigated how to get to my next destination. My experience at the train station was so unpleasant, time-consuming, and rude that I took the bus instead at the same cost and with no hassle.

Needing some serenity after these two challenges, I visited the Daoist (Taoist) Jade Emperor Temple. They were burning strange, unpleasant incense that irritated my eyes. As in Cambodia, the temples sold sparrows in small wooden cages that the adherents would buy and release to freedom, earning merit in the process. The temples would simply recapture the poor little dears and put them back in the same cages to sell again. A fitting example of religious capitalism.

The traffic is very chaotic in Saigon. Despite that, I borrowed a bicycle with my girlfriend clinging on behind me, just like so many tens of thousands of locals do. I managed the traffic with no problems. I was not counting on thieves on motorbikes.

One grabbed my girlfriend's backpack and tried to steal it. But it was not coming off her so easily. He failed, but by trying, we fell off the bicycle, causing all the surrounding bicycles to fall over, too. Her foot was injured and required medical attention. I had to take her to several doctors over the rest of the trip. Nothing was broken, but she was fairly banged up.

Haggling over everything was normal for foreigners in Vietnam, even for a glass of sugarcane juice. The Vietnamese, at least in the south as I had not traveled to the north, up to their late forties made it a point to rip off foreigners at every chance. I was used to that in Asia and India long before I arrived there. It was to the degree that they did so that was terrible.

It was common for local restaurants to charge more than the menu price showed when presenting the bill. This was the same as I experienced in Xinjiang, China. One more example suffices on this subject. An elderly woman was selling bowls of noodles to eat at small tables on the sidewalk. I asked her the price, paid her, and sat down with the other Vietnamese patrons to enjoy.

Along came a group of young dudes who asked her how much she charged me for her soup noodles. She replied that it was the same price as for everyone else. They berated and bullied her for being so stupid. These nasty idiots reminded me of the old men berating the young girl for selling me a rope at the price her father told her in the market in Kashgar, Xinjiang. The poor woman was very stressed, and the little Kashgar girl cried.

To them, it was a point of national honor to cheat foreigners. I learned enough Vietnamese to understand the basic transactions of the marketplace. This regrettable part of their culture has put them on a par with my least favorite peoples, like the Uighurs of Xinjiang and the Korean-Chinese who live in a small enclave north of the North Korea border.

After the Vietnamese War ended, a large group of refugees from the higher echelons of the military and the government fled to the US, where the government settled them all across the country. Those who were too low in the scheme of things were left behind and had to spend many years in 'reeducation' camps before they were released sometime in the 1980's.

One large group of several families settled in an old farmhouse close to where I lived on the Eastern Shore of Maryland, between Easton and Oxford. My mother, who speaks French, volunteered to help them. All educated Vietnamese spoke the language of their previous colonial masters. I was eleven years old. I accompanied her many times to their house, surrounded by a non-operating farm.

Each room housed a family or a group of single men. They were usually ex-military of the rank of captain or higher. To me, that house was like entering a different world, a very exotic one from the other side of the planet. I was fascinated by the savory smells from the large kitchen, where all the women cooked three meals a day for everyone.

The local communities across the US opened their arms to the newcomers. They donated their time and money to make the refugees welcome and to help assimilate them into their new country. Later in the 1970's when the next wave of refugees came, the so-called boat people, again various countries around the world stepped up to help them. I volunteered at the well-appointed refugee camp for them in Hong Kong when I lived there. So, perhaps it irritated me even more how they treated foreign visitors.

We took a day tour outside the city, which included the religious center of the Caodai sect. It is a strange combination of Vietnamese folk religion, Daoism, Confucianism, Buddhism, and Catholicism, founded by Ngô Văn Chiêu in 1925. This strange amalgamation includes ancestor worship, Daoist occult rituals, Confucian ethics, Buddhist karma and rebirth, and the hierarchical organization of the Catholic Church. There is a large mural in the front of the church that shows an ancient Vietnamese poet and Victor Hugo (really?) writing on a covenant tablet in Chinese and French, respectively, with Sun Yatsen (the great revolutionary who overthrew the Chinese imperial system in 1911) holding the inkwell.

There are many such syncretic religions in Asian history. One such sect, whose leader claimed he was the younger brother of Jesus, tore China apart for fourteen years from 1850 to 1864 during the Taiping Rebellion. Between twenty and thirty million died in that upheaval. The Yellow Turbin rebellion (based on secret Daoist sects) from 185 AD to 201 AD and the Boxer rebellion (practitioners of esoteric martial arts who mistakenly believed that bullets could not hurt them) at the end of the 19th century that targeted Chinese Christians and foreigners are another two examples. Falun Gong is a contemporary example.

The tour continued to a network of Vietcong tunnels from the Vietnam War; much enlarged for large tourists to visit. It was unnecessary for me to enter them, nor to read all the socialist propaganda either. I knew the history well, having lived through it as shown on the nightly news. I understood very well the great irony of the fairy tale of the time about how important it was to defend the 'free' world from the 'horrors' of socialism (of the world's Communist Parties).

The series of regimes that 58,220 US teenage boys died defending were so corrupt and dictatorial that the CIA had to take one of them out as he exceeded even the low standards of the time. I am referring to Ngo Dinh Diem, assassinated on November 2, 1963, ironically twenty days before John F Kennedy himself was assassinated. In addition, the lives of the common North Vietnamese were much better than their brothers in the south. I will go ahead and write it; they were freer too.

After Saigon, our next destination was Nha Trang, a beach city and provincial capital. The bus took twelve hours to arrive, three hours longer than it should have. I did not mind as I marveled at the non-stop, breathtaking natural beauty of coastal Vietnam. The beautiful green mountains rising to the west and rolling down into the eastern emerald sea were never boring.

Nha Trang is famous for the numerous rock formations and small islands just off the coast. Taking a boat ride among them is definitely the thing to do there. I took the all-day boat trip with the company owner and unquestionable captain of the entire operation. She originally worked in the 'service industry' with US soldiers twenty-five years before. At this time, she had a successful business and was in control of her life. We smoked cannabis together. She reminiscenced about her younger days while we floated among the small magical tropical islands. It was also my thirty-third birthday.

Capitalizing on growing foreign tourism, Vietnam had put a fence around every ruin or anything of interest, even a pleasant view of the sea, and charged an entrance fee much higher for foreigners than for locals. By this time, China had already stopped doing this. India had far more impressive ruins in the middle of fields with no fences and farmers plowing around them with their water buffalos. The Indian government did not deem them worthy of a fence, let alone of hiring someone to sell tickets.

We continued up the coast of stunning beauty to Qui Nhon, another provincial capital but much more like a small-town than Nha Trang. My girlfriend's foot became infected, so we spent a lot of time visiting doctors there. There were very few tourists there for good reason.

I chose the place because it was in the historical region of the ancient Champa Empire. They were a sea power until about 1100 AD, when they were squeezed between the Khmers from the west and the Viets from the north. Eventually, they fled by sea to various Southeast Asian destinations. They were basically a Malay-Polynesian people. Their ruins are scattered across the central coastal region.

Pho, a beef and rice noodle soup, is the national dish of Vietnam. I have prepared it a few times in recent years. It takes twenty-four hours or more, mostly to make the beef broth by boiling the bones and marrow. One can add to the finished soup various things like mint, basil, bean sprouts, and other vegetables in with the beef. There are little local pho restaurants throughout the country; one of my favorite soups from anywhere in the world.

Continuing further up the coast, we arrived at the wonderful town of Hoi An. It is an old port town revealing the various influences received from trading across Asia between the fifteenth and eighteenth centuries. Japanese and Chinese traders have left their prominent mark on the architecture. One impressive example is the 500-year-old Japanese Bridge. Its beauty will be its undoing, as it is too small to absorb the mobs of tourists who will find it soon. Then every building will become a tourist shop, restaurant, and/or guesthouse.

Canals cut through the old town. The considerable number of Chinese clan halls and temples shows their enormous influence on the city. I visited a historic house that had ironwood pillars holding up the roof. The wood is so named because of its hardness and being denser than water, which prevents it from floating. It would make a great teahouse. Cao lầu is a signature dish of the town, consisting of rice noodles, meat, greens, bean sprouts, and herbs, often served with broth made from pork and bone broth with a strong resemblance to Japanese udon.

Continuing north up the coast, we arrived at Da Nang. This port city was made famous when US President Franklin Roosevelt was asked whether after the Second World War would the US ever fight a land war in Asia again. He replied that the country would never involve itself in such a ridiculous thing: "No, the US will never go to war over some damn dingdong (Da Nang)." And yet it did, twice. Oh, well…

We visited the worthwhile Cham Museum (of the Champa civilization) in Da Nang. There I learned they revered Uroja, the Earth Mother. Uroja also means the female breast. It is that delightful womanly appendage which adorns their temple altars, pedestals, etc. The bay has a long crescent beach where white-capped waves eternally beat upon it. The Marble Mountains are five limestone outcrops with memorials to Vietcong antiaircraft gunneries and concrete Buddha statues crowning them. I did not pay the exorbitant admission fee to see that.

On the way to Hue, the bus crossed the Hai Van Pass through a spur of the Truong Son Mountain range that juts out into the South China Sea. The views were spectacular. Where the mountain meets the sea separates two long crescent beaches. There were plenty of signs of the war here. South Vietnamese bunkers and pillboxes were scattered throughout as we passed. There were no ticket sellers, only the slow process of the jungle reclaiming them.

A Lone Boatman

Vietnam 1996

Hue and the Tet Offensive

There is an enormous difference between Asian and Western beaches. If it were not for Western tourists, the beaches in Asia would be empty. A typical summer beach in North America and Europe would be covered in semi-nude, pale white, soon to be pink, bodies lying wherever they can place their towels. Without tourists, Asian beaches are pristine, empty of people and cheap kiosks.

Asians sensibly do not lie on beaches. Women would never consider lying in the sun in a bikini. They highly value white skin and would shun the suntan of a field worker. Even women fieldworkers cover themselves completely from the sun for the same reason. They are also too modest to show their bodies to all and sundry anyway.

Vietnam is known for its coffee. People drink it there with metal cups that have fine metal filters and fit over a coffee mug. They put the ground coffee in and pour hot water over it. The hot water becomes coffee as it flows through the ground beans into the mug. A metal cover keeps the water hot as it seeps through. I bought one such contraption at a market early on and used it to drink coffee for the rest of my trip.

Hue was the imperial capital of Vietnam until 1945. The emperors built it in the style of the Forbidden City in Beijing. Many lesser kingdoms surrounding ancient China copied much from Chinese culture, with Korea and Japan being notable examples. They copied clothing and architectural styles, political organization, the Confucian system of ethics, and even the written language, among other things. The emperors of Vietnam were no different.

An important thing to remember is that China controlled northern Vietnam for 1100 years, from 111 BC to 939 AD, including a brief Ming occupation from 1401 to 1428. As with many Vietnamese names like Hoi An (Hui An 會安), even the country's name is an example. The original name was Nam Việt (Nan Yue 南越) meaning south of Yue, the ancient name for Guangdong, the Chinese province directly north of Vietnam. In 1804, Emperor Gia Long reversed the two syllables to create the modern name to distance the country from the old Chinese legacy.

We wandered through the very neglected and overgrown halls and pavilions with their classical Chinese inscriptions. Though it was on a smaller scale than the Forbidden Palace in Beijing, it was certainly a virtual copy. We avoided the exorbitant entry fee at the main gate by simply entering any of the untended side gates.

As with China through the 1980's and Vietnam through the 1990's, very few local people visited any of the tourist sites, even with the much cheaper entry fees available to them. They were only interested in modern things, as bulldozers would eventually destroy anything unprotected by government fiat that did not fit that description. The government understood the economic value that tourists gave them but not the value of renovating or even maintaining their historically important sites.

From 1978 to 1979, due to Vietnam's policies against the ethnic Chinese, 450,000 of them fled either overland to southern China or by rickety boats to any neighboring country that would take them, mainly the Philippines and Thailand. Originally from Saigon and other southern cities, they were already suspect because of their connection with the recently defeated South Vietnam. They were generally very prosperous shopkeepers and business owners. Being branded as 'capitalists' did not help them either. The government confiscated all that the owners could not carry with them as donations to the new socialist reality.

Other factors included the general bad attitude many locals had against them, though they have been living in Vietnam and other Southeast Asian countries for hundreds of years. This attitude is caused mainly by the vast difference in prosperity between them and the locals. Instead of emulating their hard work, education, and ambitious business practices, it is easier to occasionally riot, kill, and destroy what they are not willing to achieve for themselves. We have seen this recently in Indonesia.

On the other hand, the ethnic Chinese did very little to integrate into the local communities. They maintain their culture and language roots from the old country. They rarely intermarry with the locals nor even take local names, except in Thailand, where the government forced them to do so in 1913. As part of the Vietnamese government's pressure on them, they were required to take Vietnamese names and citizenship.

Another factor worth noting is the conflict with their old wartime ally, China. The genocidal Khmer Rouge in Cambodia were close friends of China. Vietnam always considered this a threat. In 1978, Vietnam ended the insane regime of Pol Pot by invading Cambodia. Pol Pot fled into the jungles and continued a guerilla war until he died in 1998. China took this as a personal offense and invaded Vietnam in response. After a month of heavy losses, China withdrew in defeat. The Soviet Union revealed its impotence by failing to come to the aid of its ally, Vietnam. This did not help the cause of Vietnam's anti-Chinese domestic policies.

The old Chinatown still had many clan halls and Daoist temples. As seen by the few offerings and slight upkeep, clearly not all left. As with all old imperial capitals around the world, it was not just the imperial palace in the center of the city that sought to impress. The surrounding suburbs are full of impressive manor homes of the nobility. Of course, by now, these old suburbs are all now deeply within the confines of modern cities.

Hue was no different. The original noble families had long ago lost their property. By the time I saw them, the government had turned them into communal living quarters where a dozen or more families shared the house where originally only one lived. Many of the original Chinese clan halls and even temples were so converted. Personally, I think those are all excellent uses for them. I lived in Estoril, Portugal, in the palace where the second to last king of Romania, Carlos II, lived in exile from 1940 until his death in 1953. It was later converted from a ruin into twenty-two luxury condominiums.

Hue is famous for something else. It played a central role during the Vietcong and North Vietnamese Tet Offensive that started at the beginning of the traditional Lunar New Year celebrations, by far the biggest festival of the year. It started at the end of January 1968 and ended in their defeat three months later. As part of the offensive, they attacked hundreds of targets throughout South Vietnam, including Hue, its third largest city.

They quickly overran most of Hue, while most soldiers were on leave for the family holiday. After very bitter house to house fighting, the South Vietnamese army and US Marines finally prevailed. Besides most of the city being destroyed, over 5000 Vietcong and North Vietnamese soldiers were killed versus 668 South Vietnamese and US Marines. About 5000 civilians were also killed, including about 2000 executed by the briefly occupying army of the North. Though nothing changed on the ground in the end, the shock from the enemy's initial success did much to change US public opinion against the war.

I remember seeing an old film clip (proto videos) of the famous anthropologist, Margaret Meade, at a US Senate hearing at the capital. She became an expert on small, traditional communities in Southeast Asia and Polynesia. She promoted the idea of how much more advanced they were than us uptight Westerners with their culture of free love. As with many of her colleagues who made similar conclusions during the sexual revolution of the 1960's, this turned out to be mainly wishful thinking. They saw what they wanted to see to support their own free-swinging lifestyles, which started for some of them decades before in the 1920's and even earlier.

So, after years of futile war with so many lives and treasure wasted, US Senators had the bright idea that maybe they should learn something more about the resilient enemy other than being a bunch of pajama-wearing Marxist gooks. The hearing started with one of the senatorial worthies in his best slow Texan drawl: "So, Profeh-ssah Mee-ade, wha can yeh tell us about Vee-et Naa-ahm?"

"Excuse me, Senator, it's pronounced Vietnam (pronounced quickly just as it is spelled)"

"Lak ah sayed, profeh-ssah. Wha can yeh tell us about Vee-et Naa-ahm?" That is as far as it could go.

We decided not to continue past the old DMZ line that divided South and North Vietnam, though it was only fifty kilometers/thirty miles north of Hue. So, I never knew if the North Vietnamese were as bad as the southerners. I was exhausted from dealing with the common attitude that it was a national duty to rip off foreigners by as much as possible for even the smallest of things.

While very much looking forward to leaving Vietnam via Laos, I learned we needed exit permits. That had to be done in Da Nang. I called the Vietnam Tourism office there. They told me it would only take one US dollar and a fifteen-minute wait. I could handle that. So, the next morning, I returned to Da Nang. When I arrived at the address, it was a construction site. I had recently finished the adventures of Don Quixote, all 1064 pages. I thought I was being enchanted, as he often was.

Things quickly became closer to a Kafka story. It took me until early afternoon, after many false leads and starts, to find the real government tourist office. There they confirmed that I needed to go through a travel agent to do this. With whom was I talking on the phone the day before? I checked with several and settled on one who would take care of it all, including delivering our passports to us in Hue. It would require thirty US dollars and three days. I returned to Hue by the end of a very frustrating day, completing three trips over the same mountain pass.

The passports did arrive when they told me. I thought that was a minor miracle. We took a minibus to Khe San; the closest public transportation would go to the border town of Lao Bao. From there we continued by motorcycle taxis, each of us hanging on to the rider with our backpacks swaying behind our backs with each swerve on the rainy, wet roads.

Surprisingly, things went smoothly going through the Vietnamese side of the border. There were a few locals and no other foreigners. It became a little more complicated on the Lao side. I had to climb up to the immigration office, which was, in fact, a treehouse. There he asked me for a tip or an overtime charge, as it was Sunday. I replied that it was no problem. I would return on Monday. He laughed and let me through.

Despite the hassles and the stress of traveling through southern Vietnam, which were giving me stomach aches, I am glad I went. Besides being stunningly beautiful, it is also the location of a ridiculous war, one of the pivotal events in the history of the US when I was growing up. It was a fascinating addition to my adventures traveling through Asia.

River Fishing Traps

Laos 1996

Under Bandit Mortar Fire

Laos 1996: After entering Laos (the 's' is silent) we arrived at a border market town of some size. Fortunately, the language of Laos is basically the same as that of the Isaan region of northeast Thailand. It is so similar that the Laotian government imports its school textbooks from Thailand. Finally, as I was conversant in Thai, I could communicate without too much trouble with the locals.

Our destination for the day was Savannakhet, a large town 250 kilometers/160 miles directly west on the Mekong River and the main north-south highway. As is common in the less developed world, buses do not have a fixed schedule. They leave when the bus is sufficiently full of passengers. This could take many hours as passengers slowly fill the bus.

The two drivers of an old Soviet jeep-equivalent from the Vietnam War, thirty years before, offered to take us and one other for the same price. They would leave immediately and arrive at 1900, three hours earlier than the bus. Being the intrepid adventurer that I am, I agreed. A Japanese traveler chose to go with us, too.

We piled in the back, with me sitting in the middle. That turned out to be a terrible choice, but someone had to do it. The stick shift was right in front of me, but the rubber covering the hole around the shift from the dust of the road was so tattered that it was no longer functional. Fine dust from the dirt road blew into my face. My nose is particularly sensitive to dust. I sneezed for three days.

After a few hours, sure enough, the old jalopy broke down. As they were trying to fix it, the bus that we had shunned drove right past us, ignoring our calls to pick us up. Hours later, they managed to get the thing to work again. They dropped us off on the outskirts at 2230, and not in the center as we agreed. We found a bicycle rickshaw to take us the rest of the way to the hotel we had in mind.

The hotel was in an old, rundown French villa, with a disco occupying the entire ground floor. There was a wedding happening that night, making sleep impossible. We changed to another hotel the next day. The only memorable thing about the town was the sunset across the Mekong River, which formed the border with Thailand. Though working plumbing was always a challenge, at least the Laotians did not have the Vietnamese cultural passion to cheat foreigners at every turn.

We broke up the long trip to Vientiane by stopping at Tha Khaak. The bus was scheduled to leave at 1100 but left at 1015. So, it filled up earlier than planned. Luckily, we arrived an hour earlier at 1000 and could catch the bus. The road was good and nearly empty of other vehicles, except for a few trucks carrying timber to Thailand.

Large billboards along the highway reminded the drivers that it was built with the development funds of Australia. It is very typical of the poorer nations of the world that foreign development funds from the likes of Europe, the US, Australia, Canada, Japan, etc. pay for infrastructure, including schools and hospitals, and even most of the national budgets. Examples in the region include Laos, Cambodia, Nepal, and East Timor. In Papua New Guinea, all the higher judges are Australian. Most of sub-Saharan Africa fits into this mold.

We took the early morning bus north to the capital, Vientiane. Thanks to the well-built highway, the trip took the eight and a half hours it was supposed to. We followed the Mekong River all the way. The long Friendship Bridge connects Vientiane to Thailand. Vientiane is a happy mixture of French colonial and Buddhist styles of architecture. The city is laid out in the French way, with wide boulevards and plenty of roundabouts.

One morning, we took a tuk tuk to an outer northern suburb to visit a weaving community. There were twenty separate groups weaving the enchanting Laos style fabric. They were for sale at the Morning Market. Curiously, Laos was generally more expensive than Thailand, except for tuk tuks in Bangkok, favored by Western tourists, where they are more expensive than taxis.

Our next major destination was Luang Prabang. We first took a bus to Vang Vieng, four and a half hours north, to break up the trip. The terrain was more mountainous with more rivers than in the south. We continued along the east bank of the Mekong River. The 'bus' was a flatbed truck with a passenger compartment bolted on.

The following morning, we reached Kasi after a two-hour bus ride. Kasi is a busy market town at the crossroads of the north-south and the east-west highways. From there, we were supposed to catch the next bus north to Luang Prabang. I asked at the market where I was told that the bus had not been by in over two weeks. None were expected for quite some time due to rebel (bandit) activity on the road north.

As I pondered that bit of news, I thought perhaps we had better check in at the only guesthouse. There I met a group of a dozen Western backpackers who had been waiting for two weeks for a bus. Of course, every day they were told that it would arrive the next day, and so they waited day after day for the phantom bus.

As my readers have gathered by now, I was always creative in finding solutions. I decided I would return to the market to find a truck going north that would take us. After asking several truck drivers, I learned that they normally left in a convoy, going north after dark and arriving the next morning.

That would require us to spend a chilly night in the back of an uncomfortable truck. After a few more enquiries, I found a truck driver who agreed for 5000 kip each (925 kip to one US dollar) and would come by the guesthouse at 1600, allowing us to reach Luang Prabang by midnight. All the other drivers of the later convoy wanted 150,000 kip each!

When I returned to share the good news with the trapped backpackers that their wait was over, I was treated as a hero. Many girlfriends did not hide their annoyance with their less creative boyfriends. I solved the problem in an hour that no one in the group could do until I appeared. The truck arrived as promised, and we piled into the back, sitting on large sacks of rice. There was no roof, except for a rolled back tarp.

I leaned against the driver's cabin, taking in the incredible view of the forested hill country we were passing. A Frenchman joined me. Our girlfriends were content sitting down below, hoping the trip would end soon. He pulled out a bottle of tequila, and we became good buddies as we passed the bottle between us.

We passed several army checkpoints with the driver's unusual cargo hidden out of sight. Soon there were no checkpoints. We had entered bandit country. As I wrote earlier, many countries around the world do not control their border areas. Some do not even control extensive areas in the interior. We were now in one of those countries.

I assumed the local driver knew the situation well. Even so, he took a chance to make some extra money. Just as it became too dark to see well, with us hunkered down below the sides of the truck among the sacks, we came under mortar fire from the unseen bandits. They missed, but the nearby explosions were enough of a reminder that we might not be in the right place at the right time.

The driver must have surprised them as he sped past. They would have made him pay the unofficial tax to use 'their' road if they were prepared. They were expecting the regular convoy many hours later. If they did stop the driver, they might have taken a few sacks of rice with them and then noticed us. Well, well, what do we have here?

The heavy truck did its best to speed past and onward to safety. Sometime later, it poured rain. The driver stopped and covered us with the tarp. But we became quite drenched anyway. We stopped at a lone restaurant by the road for a quick meal. There was a sizeable open fire behind the restaurant. There, I took off my shirt and jacket to dry them by the fire. I was freezing, but was determined not to be wet, too.

A few hours later, we finally arrived shortly after midnight as scheduled. The driver was kind enough to take us to a hotel in the center, which had enough rooms for all of us. The next morning, we went our separate ways.

Luang Prabang was the original royal capital until 1975, when the Marxist/socialist Pathet Lao took over and abolished the monarchy. It is a very pleasant city at the confluence of the Mekong and the Nan Khan rivers. The city is full of old palaces and Buddhist temples (wats, as they are also called in Thailand). The most impressive temple is Wat Xieng Thong, built in 1560. It is a magnificent masterpiece of design and proportion.

Considering the arduous trip to get there, it was well worth it. The tequila-sharing couple we met on the truck joined us on our wandering around the city. We had after dinner tea in our room. He left me with a fair amount of herb from a woman at the Vientiane Morning Market who had tried to sell it to me earlier.

We visited a lacquerware workshop. I bought a wood and paper umbrella with a beautiful scene of storks and clouds. I never used it as an umbrella, though it would have functioned well with its waterproof lacquered paper. It is now in my house in Portugal, hanging upside down from the ceiling, covering the light in my 'Asian' room full of various things from my Asian travels. The light shining through makes for an enchanting effect.

Our final destination was Xiangkhouang Province in the northeast. After our experience traveling to Luang Prabang, we decided to fly there. A small, seventeen-seater Chinese built plane took us there on the forty-minute flight. We shared the flight with a Brit, a Frenchman, and a New Zealand family with three children.

Though the province is also mountainous, we visited the rolling grasslands of the plateau. This lightly populated province is also home of the UNESCO recognized Plain of Jars, the most important megalithic site in Southeast Asia. We stayed in a village in the center of the area. I organized tuk tuks to take us all out to several sites of jars in the surrounding barren hills.

The jars are one to three meters tall (three to ten feet) and were carved from rock around 1000 BC. There are over ninety sites with between one and four hundred rock jars. Most were carved from rocks originally at the sites, but some were hauled from quarries eight kilometers/five miles away. They served as burial urns. These huge rock urns scattered in clusters around the barren countryside was a surreal sight.

Xiangkhouang Province is famous for something else. It is considered the most heavily bombed area on Earth. It gained this dubious distinction by the results of heavy carpet bombing by the US Airforce B-52 bombers during the Vietnam War from 1964 to 1969. The US supported the Royalist faction led by its Hmong general, fighting against the Pathet Lao in the province. Of the 262 million anti-personnel cluster bombs dropped, about 80 million did not explode and remain a deadly danger. New Zealand is funding the ongoing efforts to find and remove them.

Back then, it was still common to use terms like First World and Third World to distinguish between the developed and the less developed worlds. I created a system that fleshed out that overly simple system. Countries that were well on their way to the First World, I called the Second World. There were those who were still very far behind, which I called the Fourth World. Then there were those few countries that had not yet decided to join the world economic order and lived in their own strange realities. I named them the Fifth World.

In the mid-1990's, North America, Japan, and Western Europe fit in the First World. Taiwan and South Korea were examples of the Second. Thailand, India, Malaysia, and the Philippines were examples of the Third World. China and Vietnam were examples of the Fourth World. Countries like Burma, Cambodia, Laos, and Nepal were examples of the Fifth World. These definitions have obviously changed greatly over the years. Perhaps only countries like Cuba and North Korea still constitute the Fifth World.

We flew back to Vientiane and returned to Bangkok overland. We stopped at the Isan cities of Udon Thani and Khon Kaen in northeast Thailand. Udon Thani is large enough to have a US consulate. I walked past it on the way to somewhere else. Outside the consulate were several old US veterans of the Vietnam War collecting their monthly social security payments. They all had teenage Thai wives with babies. One was even driving his own tuk tuk. They had decided to live there after the war, enjoying the good but simple lifestyle a US pension can afford in a laid back Southeast Asian agricultural province.

We visited an ancient burial site nearby that was 5000 years old. The ancients buried their dead in clay pots that they had painted with artistic swirls around the outside. It was very modern in its effect. We returned by hitchhiking in the back of a pickup truck. Another Thai was doing the same. It turned out he had lived eighteen years in Lille, France. He was married to a French woman and had two children. We spoke French all the way back.

We took the overnight train to Bangkok, sitting next to three Buddhist monks and three Thai Catholic nuns. Surprisingly, they ignored each other. We spent a week visiting friends and preparing for our trip eastward by buying our plane tickets to San Francisco with a two-week stopover in Taiwan.

In Taiwan, we visited family and friends, recovering from our tiring but fulfilling trip through Nepal, India, Cambodia, Vietnam, and Laos that lasted six months. It was a historic time to be in Taiwan. The country was in full campaign mode for the national elections, the first free one in the history of the Chinese people anywhere (including Singapore).

There were many political parties with their campaign offices scattered throughout the city. One of them really caught my eye. It was the Communist Party headquarters! Then I realized just how free the elections were. The US Navy ship Independence and the aircraft carrier Nimitz patrolled the Taiwan Straits to prevent any interference by China. It was also when the very modern Taipei city overhead metro system opened, operating with no drivers.

Most of my remaining time there I spent contemplating the end of this chapter of living in Asia and starting my new life in the US, a life I would have to invent after I arrived. I had the luxury of choosing anywhere in the country to live, so I chose San Francisco, my favorite US city. I would later return to live and work in Asia for many more years, but that is a subject for a later time.

An Asian Kitty

1997

Oakland, California

Oakland, California 1996 to 1999

A Life of Service to Others

After so many years of traveling, working, and living in Asia, it was time for me to return to the US and start a new chapter in my life. But what exactly? I still had no concrete plan or path, just various ideas. There was, however, an overarching ideal. I decided I would live in service to others. I wanted to live as close to the ideals of Jesus, a hero of mine, as I could.

Of all the places in the US I could have chosen, I chose San Francisco, as it was always my favorite US city. Because of the high cost of renting in that wonderful city, we ended up across the San Francisco Bay, in Oakland. An ex-boyfriend of a childhood compatriot friend of my Taiwanese girlfriend, who could never refuse any man she met, offered us to stay in his flat he was renting in an office building in the city center.

He was a typical modern, dysfunctional stoner dude of the post-hippy era with all the attitudes that implies, including free love and never working for the 'man'. He had a reasonably sophisticated and hydroponic noble herb operation occupying a large part of the flat. His flat occupied the entire fourth floor of the office building. As he explained to me, because of him occupying a commercial space, the police could never track his high electricity consumption for all the heat lamps. Unusually high electricity usage was a tip-off for police to find such entrepreneurs.

Curtains divided the space of the large wall less flat into bedrooms and the other rooms of a normal apartment. He had an old beat-up car with doors that could not lock. With a very coveted dedicated parking spot in the city center, he made a deal with a homeless man, whom he often found sleeping in his car. He could sleep in the car out of the elements as long as he did not urinate or defecate in it. Of course, he would have to leave the car when my friend needed it.

Together, we went on a ten-day Vipassana meditation retreat on top of a heavily forested mountain in the exact geographic center of California, at North Fork near Fresno. We took the train to Fresno and back. Organizers of the retreat took care of the remaining distance from the train station. The daily schedule started at 0400 and ended at 2200. The day was full of meditation, lectures, and much time alone reflecting on the higher truths. We had only two simple meals a day. A very important requirement was that we remained in silence for the whole ten days.

If we ignore deities with their legends and fairy tales, we could experience there the essential similarities between Buddhism and Hinduism. By concentrating on emptying our minds and removing all agendas, we can suppress the ego. By suppressing our egos, we can step outside the 'I' and identify with everything and everyone else around us. After this experience, I can say that I became Enlightened in the Buddhist sense. I knew the reality of life and the ultimate truths of the Spirit and the Cosmos.

The ultimate goal is Liberation when we free ourselves of all cravings and fears. We would have an equanimous mind with no attachments, attractions or aversions. This is the part I could never wrap my mind around. Love being such an important part of my life, I could not treat everyone equally. One cannot love everyone equally. Besides family and friends, there are those whom we love romantically. I cannot accept there being no distinction between beauty and ugliness. So, I remain enlightened but not liberated.

After ten days of silence, the sounds of people around us on the train returning to Oakland were deafening. It took me a few days to accept any noise above a whisper. There was a young and beautiful but troubled couple who were staying at the same flat in Oakland as we were, friends of our host, whom I came to know. They also attended the retreat. They drove down and then left early by a day. Obviously, they learned nothing. As soon as they started driving away, they took their drugs of choice. They crashed on the way back and both died. I am glad they did not offer us a ride.

I found an excellent apartment on the other side of Lake Merritt from the city center, a ten-minute walk away. My apartment was on the second and highest floor of a four-unit building. There were four such buildings in a row along the quiet street. We each had a garage in the back of the buildings.

The buildings were about 100 years old, built of stone. It was a time when people ate in large dining rooms. I turned that into my home office with a large L-shaped desk. The equally large living room included a small dining table, making it our dining room, too. We turned the smaller bedroom into a study for my girlfriend, leaving the larger one for us. A door from the kitchen led to a wooden stairway that connected to the back street below and to the roof above. From the roof, we could watch the July Fourth fireworks over the lake. We had windows on all four sides.

The apartment buildings were just a few doors away from the main road, where Little Saigon stretched for many blocks south. The food markets were more reasonably priced compared to the bustling China Town in the center of the city. Our landlords were a couple from Hong Kong. They did not speak English so well. We could communicate in Mandarin with no problem, which gave them no end of a pleasant surprise.

The Vietnamese immigrants lived a few blocks further west. Where I lived was almost all Afro-American. I was the only Euro-American I ever saw in that area. All my neighbors were very cool, hard-working, professional families. I became quite close to three such families.

The married couple across from me were very friendly. He worked at a dentist supply company in San Francisco. He had a serious belching problem we could hear through the thick walls of our apartments. I introduced him to a Chinese herbal medicine, which I knew would work. It did, much to his delight. They invited us to their big wedding anniversary party in a community hall. It was full of friends and family. I was the only Euro-American there. I was honored.

The couple below were originally from Texas. He worked at the San Francisco Public Library. They had a son in his late teens who was mentally disabled and one of the nicest people one would ever meet. My friend made Texas barbecue with mesquite wood to add its particular flavor to the pulled pork. He always gave me a big plate. We played chess and smoked the noble herb in front of my garage with the door open.

The other couple lived in the neighboring apartment building across from the small side walkway that separated the buildings. He was a salesman at a furniture store and married with younger children. He invited me to a party at a house with many of his friends further south in the city. Again, I was the only Euro-American there and was honored to be among them.

There was a network where a homeless or otherwise struggling person could get a free hot meal at least once a day, whether it was at the Catholic Church, or the Synagogue, or somewhere else. One could see a doctor for non-emergencies (may the gods help someone with an emergency) at various locations in the Bay Area at certain times of the week. One could get dental care from the students at the dental school in San Francisco (they needed the practice).

After moving out of my house in Thailand, I stored all my things with a moving company in Bangkok. They shipped the twenty-foot container to my apartment in Oakland. The moving company on the US side that partnered with the one in Bangkok cleared US Customs but held my shipment until I paid their bogus invoice. I had paid for everything, door-to-door, to the Thai company. I had the contract and the invoices to prove it.

As with these free services, there was a free legal service provided by volunteer lawyers to help in various minor civil cases. I remember we met in a room at the Oakland Public Library. He asked me several times: "What would make me whole?" My day in court arrived. It all proved useless. Despite all my paperwork proving otherwise, the judge ruled in favor of the moving company. I had to pay a second time to get my things delivered. This shows that rather than relying on the kindness of volunteer strangers, it is far better to have a humane public services system.

There often was a pale, thin woman who looked like she was in her forties, but was probably in her late twenties, hanging out at the street corner a few steps from my apartment building. I hardly noticed the first time I passed her. She spoke in a raspy low voice, if I would kindly bed her for fifty dollars. I stopped and stared at her, not immediately grasping what she was offering.

She misunderstood me and repeated her proposition, but with a quick drop in rent to twenty-five dollars. As I shook my head and continued my walk, she called after me with a price of fifteen dollars. If she had been more genteel and classy, I would have gladly paid fifteen dollars for her to have a decent lunch with me.

I tried to be as self-sufficient as I could by making my own bagels, doufu (tofu), bread, etc. I bought the heavily discounted fruit from the Vietnamese market that was very close to retiring. This overripe fruit was perfect for making fruit wine.

After I settled in, I considered how to best serve my community and the less well-off. I hit upon the most stressful occupation after policemen walking the streets of the inner cities: to teach in the Oakland public school system as a substitute teacher. The stress comes from trying to teach children who do not want to learn and try to get away with anything with an adult who was only there temporarily.

The most important thing about being a teacher is to control the classroom. Actual teaching is in a distant second place. I learned very early on that ten percent of the students get it and are there to learn no matter what happens around them. Another ten percent of the students have no interest in learning and will disrupt the class at every chance they can. The other eighty percent will follow whichever group is in the ascendant. That is why it is paramount to control the class, so the middle eighty percent become influenced by the serious ten percent.

The secretaries at the office were always annoyed with me because after giving certain badly disruptive kids many chances, I would throw them out of class and send them there. Sometimes I sent six or seven to the office. This tactic was very successful in winning over the middle eighty percent. I especially enjoyed teaching kindergarten and first grade. The little dears were not yet old enough to have their own independent personalities. By the second grade, it was all over.

Later, I also taught for a while in Southern California. Once I taught at a school specifically for teenage gangbangers. There were metal detectors throughout, and no gang colors or symbols could be worn. All the teachers were men in their thirties, much bigger and tougher than normal. I fit that description then.

The principal, bigger and tougher than all of us, told me at the beginning of class to make sure that two particular students had no chance of coming into contact with each other. My classroom was completely full of middle teenagers who probably had seen it all by the time they were fifteen. The space between the rows made it very difficult to walk between them. The room had doors on three sides.

One of these malcontents was sitting in the back corner, and the other was sitting in the front at the opposite corner. As I was teaching, someone said something, and the one in the back must have flown over the six filled seats in front of him and viciously attacked the one in the front. Immediately all three doors burst open, and three of my fellow teachers rushed in, pulled them apart, and took them out of the classroom. The whole thing happened within a minute. I was shocked.

At the end of the day, the principal called me into his office. I was expecting the worst since I had done the one thing a teacher should never do: I lost control of the classroom. To my shock, he tried every way he could to convince me to join them full time, including the highest pay possible, etc. I thanked him for his kind consideration and never returned.

Note: I did not take any photos while I lived in Oakland. I was there to live my experiences and not record them.

Lighthouse off the Coast

Oakland, California 1996 to 1999

Teaching in the Public Schools

I taught almost every subject in every grade in nearly every public school in Oakland. I taught in reform schools (prisons for youth offenders with gates, bars, and guards with guns) and in orphanages with teenagers who never had a family nor even knew their parents. Most of the time, I was the proverbial Dutch boy who stuck his finger in the daily leak in the dike. The schools sent me to teach whatever was in most serious need. I worked every day.

Often it was math class. Besides there being very few men teachers, only about fifteen percent of the total, there was a serious shortage of teachers of any kind. All too often, math class meant someone wheeled a video player into the classroom. The students were supposed to watch and learn from that.

The school district designated me as an emergency credentialed teacher, which meant that I had taken an exam to prove I knew more than the students. I also had to pass an extensive FBI background check to make sure I was safe to be in the same room as minors. I also had to have some kind of degree, which my MBA satisfied. That was it.

Soon the school district decided I would be great as a specialist teaching special needs students (special ed), those with mental disabilities, and as an alternative education specialist (alt ed). Alt ed meant that I taught students who had lost significant class time due to being incarcerated or being pregnant and caring for an infant.

Later, when I taught in southern California, it was cool for the girls to date a boy who had recently left juvenile hall with their very short crew cut hair, military style. So, all the boys had the same haircut, whether or not they were ever in juvenile hall.

I remember I had two girls in one of my classes. They were fifteen years old and were discussing a birthday party one was having for her second child. Her friend had two babies, too.

I was in no way a specialist in either. What I did have that many other teachers did not was a strong dedication to serving the children. From this, I had a vast reservoir of patience and care. I had the opportunity to influence and indeed change the individual lives of some of these young people, who generally come from weak families and are normally ignored by society. Many, if not most, had little or no interaction with an adult man. Many had never met their fathers.

The following experiences will answer the question: why do people teach in the difficult public schools of large US cities?

I was teaching a group of alt ed students in their mid-teens. It was a reading class. We sat in a circle, and each read a paragraph from the same book out loud. When it was a certain Latino boy's turn to read, he refused. The worse than useless teacher's assistant told me to move on and not to waste my time with him. He never reads.

I replied that I was there to help these kids learn how to read. So, I told the boy that we would read the story together, just he and I. We started reading together. After a while, I stopped and let him continue on his own. He continued reading paragraph after paragraph on his own for the first time. I only stopped him after he had read a few pages. He had finally found the confidence to read. Why? Because he had a teacher who cared and did not simply write him off, as the assistant did.

I taught math for a while at a high school that was roughly half Latino and half Afro-American. The school often had to go into lockdown when the two groups started brawling in the halls. Every classroom had a phone for the teacher to use in emergencies. No one had cell phones then. There were always students who would try to sneak behind the teacher's back and use the phone to call their friends outside. A Latina did that when I was busy with other students. A rare fellow male teacher walked by and saw her through the open door. He came in to stop her. Holding the heavy phone receiver in her hand, she hit him hard in the face with it. That stupid action was considered an assault. The police came in to handle it. Many of these kids had serious anger issues.

In this same class, I was teaching how to do arithmetic with mixed fractions, which required finding the common denominator. I explained in detail at the blackboard (with chalk) and then told them to do the exercises in the textbook. I walked among them to see how they were doing.

One girl stared blankly at the page, doing nothing. Obviously, she needed my personal attention. So, I sat beside her and explained again. I did a few problems as examples. Then I let her try them. After helping her more, she finally grasped it and could do the exercises on her own. As I rose to continue helping others, she told me how shocked she was that a teacher would spend time helping her. Normally, the regular teachers would tell the students to do certain pages in the textbook while they read the newspaper, ignoring them.

I taught at another high school for the last four months of the school year, a class on how to prepare for the working world. They were juniors, so they were sixteen and seventeen years old, old enough to work over the summer vacation. The class included subjects like how to find jobs, how to answer job postings in the newspaper, how to do interviews, how to create a resume (CV), etc.

Each student had a desktop computer with Word. They had to write their resumes according to the standard format of the time. The classroom had a printer, so I could print them out for the students to use when I decided they were ready.

My classroom was in the far corner of the school grounds, in a temporary building. Often a group of huge Afro-American boys who towered over me would sneak out of their classes and come to mine to talk with one of their buddies in my class. Of course, I had to throw them out and send them back to their classrooms. This was something they did not want to do and were curious how I would make them.

The fundamental difference between boys and men is self-confidence. I had that in abundance. I would not back down until they left on their own. Their buddy in question was a product of his community. It was common for the boys to wear gold (plated) symbols made into a type of a metal frame that they could fit over the front two teeth. His were dollar signs. Is that still a thing?

He clearly had never written anything in his life. A resume was way beyond him. So, as usual, I sat down next to him, and we did it together. He wanted to find a summer job at the county fair. Months later, at the end of the school year, he hugged me, telling me I was the best teacher he had ever had.

In that same class, a pretty Latina called me 'guapo' every time she entered the classroom. It is Spanish for 'handsome'. She had an interesting story, more so than usual. She was sixteen then and originally from Los Angeles. Her mother's boyfriend was hitting on her (heavy flirting). What would any single mother do in such a situation? Obviously, she would kick her daughter out onto the street. She ended up living in a small room in the back of a Mexican restaurant in the Latino community in south Oakland, 1000 kilometers/600 miles north of Los Angeles. The owners fed her and let her stay there in exchange for washing dishes and cleaning the restaurant. I sure hope she was able to find a good life for herself.

The Reserve Officers' Training Corps (ROTC) offices in the high schools always shocked me. These were recruitment offices for the US military, mainly the army. Maybe about ten percent of the students joined. They did drills and maybe shot rifles (.22 caliber). About once a week, they appeared in class in their military uniforms. This is just one example of how militaristic the US is, sharing the same militarism as China, Russia, and the few socialist countries left.

Another example is how common it is to see bumper stickers with the words "Proud Parent of an Army Soldier" or "Proud Parent of a Marine". I was on a consulting project once (decades later) in Ohio. A British colleague and I were driving to the client's factory. He told me that in the UK it would be considered a huge disgrace to be such a parent because it meant that the best he could do to prepare his son for life was for him to enter the military.

Once my senior class joined several others at an event at the University of California, Berkeley. I had the chance to talk with several students about their after-graduation plans. An Afro-American girl told me rather reluctantly she was not sure but would probably go into the military. I asked her why. She replied because she wanted to see the world.

I have heard that too often, including in military recruitment propaganda. Military bases, almost without exception, are in the worst, most boring, and remote parts of a country. I told her there were other options for doing that. With her complete attention, I explained what the Peace Corps was. It is a US government program where young people can volunteer to work on development projects in many of the less developed countries around the world for a few years. She had never heard of it. I told her there was a recruitment office at the university and showed her where it was in the next building. She went and most certainly had a much more positive life experience for it.

It was not all about the students. Once while taking a rest in the teachers' break room, I overheard my fellow teachers, who were all young women my age, talking about a private party they were organizing. The party sponsor was a salesman of sexual wares who would present the wide range of his company's products, including provocative clothing, various hand tools, and other paraphernalia for such purposes. They needed a male model and asked me to be him. I was in my mid-thirties and in top physical shape. I was also flattered. Who says schoolteachers are boring?

So, with all these positive experiences with the students, why did I eventually end this mission of service to my community? One reason was the school district administration, which occupied an entire city block with its enormous office building. They treated the teachers like students.

I came to a high school once and checked my school mail, which was put in open wooden cubby spaces near the school's office. I could see that each teacher received the same notice, as every cubby space had a sheet of paper extending from it. There were at least fifty or more sheets of paper for that many teachers. They all had the same thing printed with a single sentence: "Teachers, please conserve paper."

For four months, while I taught the juniors how to prepare for work life, I could not get a room key from the school. Every morning, I had to find the janitor to unlock the door. When I asked to have my own key, they told me it would take more than a year to receive one from the incredibly bureaucratic headquarters.

The last straw happened when I was teaching fourth graders (ten-year-olds). At the end of the day, the principal called me into her office. Clearly, I was in trouble. She informed me that a girl from my class had told her I had said something very inappropriate to the little girl. This was a major fireable offense, if not criminal. It was especially offensive because I was a Euro-American man teaching in an Afro-American school. I asked what it was that I supposedly said. At first, she did not want to tell me but finally did.

Allegedly, I told the little girl, "My, I'd like to jive that booty." I replied that I had no idea what that meant. Whatever it was, it simply was not in my vocabulary. I would not even know how to say that sentence. The principal was an Afro-American woman herself and understood the logic of my predicament. A little girl knew how to get her teacher into trouble. Though the complaint went into my record as required by law, she allowed me to write by hand in front of her my defense, which she then stapled to the child's accusation. Nothing further happened, but that was enough to drive me away.

In a primary school, I taught first graders simple English. The school allowed parents to sit in class with them (mothers, in fact). She tried to help her little son, but the unfortunate fact was that he knew English better than she did. I was teaching her more than him.

Oakland was the epicenter of the bizarre idea of Ebonics. It had fallen away just a few years before I arrived. Basically, the idea was that Afro-Americans spoke a proper dialect of English that should not only be respected but taught in the public schools. What dialect did poor Euro-American kids speak? Rather than teach them proper English, the idea was to respect and make respectable bad English.

Many Afro-Americans believe that to be articulate with proper English is to 'talk white'. I have seen efforts by more intelligent people from that community to demonstrate the fallacy of that ridiculous attitude. Speaking bad English does not help them find a career path and make their way in the world. All my neighbors in Oakland were professionals, and all spoke proper English.

California Coast

1998
Oakland, California

Oakland, California 1996 to 1999

Becoming a Bicycle Mechanic

When entering the main entrance hall of many schools in the more predominately Afro-American communities, one faced four enormous portraits hanging on each of the four walls. They were portraits of Martin Luther King Jr. (another personal hero), Marcus Garvey, Malcolm X, and Booker T. Washington. It reminded me exactly of what I had seen in the great halls of the People in Beijing. Except there, they were Mao Zedong, Karl Marx, Vladimir Lenin, and Friedrich Engels.

Public education has become too politicized since I was a student. Those portraits and the Ebonics movement are examples. I was dismayed in English classes that anything written by a male Euro-American author was nowhere to be seen. All the books were written by Afro-Americans, preferably women, with a few by Latino authors in their respective communities. The times were still before the gay and lesbian movement became a thing. Nowadays, public schools must include them in English classes, too.

I understand the intent is to show the students that it is possible for authors from their communities to be successful, to be well educated, and able to write moving prose. They were role models. It also limited their world by never giving them the opportunity to read great literature of their nation, like Mark Twain, Ernest Hemingway, John Steinbeck, etc. The worthy goal of exposing students to great literature has become subservient to socio-political objectives.

Since I followed the principles of living simply, I walked or took public transportation everywhere. Those methods were limiting, so

I added a third means of getting around: bicycling. Instead of buying one, I learned how to be a bicycle mechanic and built my own.

I met Richard, an elderly hippie and odd tinker, who lived in a room under the steps of an apartment building in Berkeley. He had a cot in a corner surrounded by a large inventory of used bicycle parts, without a bathroom or running water. His girlfriend, another elderly hippie, house sat for people while they were away for whatever reason and needed someone to water the plants and take care of the cats. He stayed with her when she had those gigs.

This is an example of how many of his fellows thought. He was sixty-four and could start collecting Social Security in the following year. The requirement is that one must have worked for ten years, forty quarters, at some kind of job, whether self-employed or not, that paid taxes into the system. He only worked, according to the government's definition, for thirty-eight quarters. I told him to find a job, any job, for six months so he would be eligible for at least that steady income from a retirement pension and maybe be able to live in a place with running water. This he would not do.

Berkeley was full of these hippies who were in their sixties and seventies. More than a dozen would always turn up as a group at all the city festivals in the nude. It was not a pretty sight, but I had to agree with their free spirits.

He traveled around the world in the late 1950's. So, we had traveling in common. For several hours every afternoon, he taught me how to be a bicycle mechanic. In addition, I took classes at the Berkeley Bicycle Cooperative and read extensively about gear ratios and the like. He and I assembled bicycles from all the various parts he had lying around his living space and frames hanging from hooks throughout. During this time, I built my own to the exact gear ratio that would help me up the Oakland hills with an old Mercier French racing frame. That was my main means of transportation.

I joined a local bicycle club, the Oakland Yellow Jackets, and rode on their group rides. I also often rode for half a day across the Oakland hills to the flatlands of eastern California and back. On one such ride, returning through southern Oakland, I passed the Hells Angels headquarters (an infamous motorcycle gang) and further on the headquarters of the Black Panthers. Founded in the 1960's, they caused quite a scandal with Euro-Americans when they organized social programs for their communities in Oakland and legally armed themselves to protect against the real threat of the police and Hoover's FBI. Their crime was being poor, organized, and armed while being black.

Breaking down far from home with no cell phone (still in its infancy) was never a concern. I carried in a small pouch connected to the back of my saddle (bicycle seat) all the tools necessary for almost any contingency. Inside that pouch was even a little tool called 'the third hand', which is absolutely necessary to fix a broken chain. I had to use it once. Flat tires were a simple five-minute hassle.

Riding down the hills over eighty kilometers/fifty miles per hour was exhilarating. I never thought of the insanity of doing that while following the many twists and turns of narrow roads. Usually, I had only the width of the line that separated the main driving area from the embankments and forest to ride on. I would soon learn the folly of this.

Once, as I had just started accelerating down the steep hill to the city, my derailleur bent into the spokes of my rear wheel. A derailleur is the mechanism that changes the gears (cogs) of the rear gear cassette. The result was as if the neighborhood bully jammed a stick into your back spokes as you were riding by when you were a child (yes, it happened to me). The bicycle would immediately stop, and the rider would fall off. According to the laws of physics, the bicycle stops moving, but the rider continues forward at the original speed.

Right behind me was a large Mercedes SUV. If I had fallen that way, I would have been hit by that. So, I decided to fall into the embankment on the other side. As I fell, I hit the back of my head. Fortunately, I had enough sense to wear a bicycle helmet. The design of such a helmet is to spread the force of the impact around the helmet and away from the head. I felt that force spread around my head like someone gently laid their hands on my head, as the helmet did its job. I would have died otherwise.

The results were a damaged bicycle, a destroyed helmet, and a broken right wrist. I was still an hour's ride away from my apartment. I was badly banged up and could not walk for the several hours it would take. Incredibly, a woman who was driving behind me saw all of this. She stopped and loaded me and my useless bicycle into her car and drove me to her place nearby. There we took stock to see if I was alright enough to not need an ambulance. I was, and she drove me to my place. What a great Good Samaritan!

I managed to drive myself to a hospital where they x-rayed me, put a cast on my broken wrist, and sent me on my way. I learned how to write with my left hand. It was probably better than my normal handwriting, which is atrocious, a product of rebellion in my second grade.

It only takes an impact to the head at a speed of twenty kilometers/fourteen miles per hour to be fatal. An impact at half that speed can cause severe and permanent brain trauma. Most people comfortably ride at seventeen kilometers/ twelve miles per hour on average. I knew a young man who drank too much at a friend's party, rode his motorcycle around the friend's yard without a helmet, and crashed into a tree, though he was going quite slowly. I had lunch with him once. He could not put a fork of food into his mouth. Food was all over his face as he tried. So, dear readers, ALWAYS WEAR A HELMET!!!

The Oakland Yellow Jackets organized a century ride from San Francisco to Monterey on the Pacific coast to the south. A century ride is so named for the distance of 100 miles (160 kilometers). This ride was 120 miles/190 kilometers. We rode there as a group, following the Pacific Coast Highway. We spent the night and returned the next day. Because we needed about 5000 calories to exert ourselves that far (only 2500 calories are required for a normal day), the club organized rest stops along the way, manned by volunteers with food and drink so we could make it to our destination.

I did this ride only a few weeks after my cast was removed. Still, the vibration of the road into my just healed right wrist was so painful, I had to ride with just my left hand on the handlebar and my right one hanging down beside me. Certainly, I would not let something so minor as that interfere with my bicycling.

As usual, I read a lot. In this phase, I read authors such as Henry David Thoreau (the best-known Natural Mystic Man of the US, another personal hero), Carl Jung, Joseph Campbell, Nikos Kazantzakis, etc. Kazantzakis, who is famous for Zorba the Greek and The Last Temptation of Christ, wrote many other great works besides. I particularly enjoyed his The Odyssey: A Modern Sequel.

The story begins after Odysseus returned home from the Trojan War and all his misadventures of years attempting that. After living some decades in the comfort of his home and family, he became bored. He gathered his old shipmates and sailed off again for one last adventure. The goal of his final voyage is to find the elusive meaning of life.

He wrote the story in the same style as the original, as a grand epic poem. Of all the wonderful wisdom this book reveals, two things stand out. First, the ancient Greeks believed mankind was greater than the gods because we have free choice. We can change our lives and ourselves if we choose. The gods cannot. Though they have immortality, they cannot change anything about themselves. The God of War cannot wage peace, nor can the God of Peace wage war. They are cast in an unbreakable mold.

The second is about our perception of the gods in general. There are four stages through which Mankind must pass in his understanding of the nature of the divine. They are as follows:

First, good and evil are enemies, the belief of most religions.

Second, good and evil are co-workers.

Third, good and evil are one, the belief of most mystics, East or West.

Fourth, this 'one' does not exist, the belief of some mystics of the East and me.

When I read that, I knew he and I were kindred spirits. Good and evil are human constructs. We call it morality. We humans need morality to coexist in communities. Since I consider myself a civilized person, I abide by morality too. As for the gods, they are neither good nor evil. They just are. I prefer to combine them all into one and call that the Spirit. One may call it the Holy Spirit or the Great Spirit, or whatever. This Spirit does not 'do'. It simply 'is'. With this, one can ignore the eternal question of why an all-powerful, good god allows bad things to happen to good people and vice versa.

California Seals Basking on a Beach

Oakland, California 1996 to 1999

A Quaker Life

I became a member of the Religious Society of Friends (Quakers) at the 57th Street Meeting in Hyde Park when I was nineteen years and a student at the University of Chicago. We meet in silence, without the hierarchy of preachers and all the rest. Though we have principles of living, we do not have a fixed creed like a bible. The Spirit reveals Itself to humanity throughout all time in various ways.

Most people know us from our social activism, including our testimony of non-violence and speaking truth to power. Just one of many examples is the American Friends Service Committee and the Friends Service Council of the UK jointly won the Nobel Peace Prize in 1947 for their "pioneering international peace work and their compassionate efforts to alleviate human suffering and promote fellowship between nations". They organized efforts to help the starving and traumatized civilian populations of Europe after the Second World War.

Much of this help went to the ex-Axis countries, particularly Germany, where there was the most need, having been almost completely destroyed from one end to the other. There, most people were homeless and starving. These are two of the main Quaker organizations striving for peace and social justice. Because of their efforts to ease the misery of the German people, they were heavily criticized for aiding and abetting the already surrendered enemy by many across the political spectrum. During my time, they were criticized for helping the wounded of the Vietnam War with ambulance and medical field services, regardless of which side they were on.

All people, indeed all living beings, have a divine light burning within their hearts. We meet in silence with no agenda. With empty minds, we wait for the Spirit to fill our hearts with a brighter light so that we can carry it forth into the world, trying to make it a better place than when we found it. It is a mystical group, but unlike the practice of Eastern religions, we seek the Spirit not just for ourselves as individuals, but for all of us together as a community.

I joined my local Quaker Meeting, Strawberry Creek. We met at a primary school on the Oakland side of the border with Berkeley. It was a large group of people from across all segments of life, including families with children and many from the LGBT community. The Meeting chose me to be the Clerk of the Peace and Social Concerns Committee. In this role, I managed to persuade the committee members to focus on the problems we see outside our doors every day, like homelessness, rather than helping the barefoot children of Bolivia. I took a particular interest in teen homelessness.

This fit in perfectly with my life of service to others. We worked to construct a ladder, connecting the various services that already existed. The first step on the ladder was to have a warm and safe place to sleep for the night, where one could shower and wash one's clothes. The next step was an affordable community with private rooms and living with strict rules, especially regarding drugs and alcohol. The ladder continued until eventually arriving at the last step, with a place of one's own and a regular job.

Through this effort, I became very familiar with their plight. The problem of teen homelessness was caused mainly by a child running away from abusive or nonexistent homes. Drug use and prostitution may or may not be involved. Adult homelessness is usually caused by mental illness and substance abuse. Because of the non-existent healthcare system in the US, these people cannot afford the medication they need. If they do manage to get some medication through a special program or another, it is usually only enough for a few weeks out of the month for the short time the public money lasts. This medication should never be taken with other drugs or alcohol. But they do anyway.

Without sleeping or eating well for years, they are physically weak. The public often sees them as filthy, stinking, pushing a shopping cart full of random things while raving into the wind. People fear them rather than try to help them. We helped them and knew them as individuals. It was always a great tragedy when, as was often the case, one of them was moving up the ladder to independence and then seeing him fall back down.

That homelessness exists at all is a great crime. It is not at all a problem of affordable housing. It is a problem of a society that does not care about the most vulnerable and weakest of its citizens. In reality, it is a society where people do not really care about each other. Universal healthcare, including mental health, and safe housing are universal human rights, as clearly written in the United Nations document, the Universal Declaration of Human Rights. Ironically, the US played a key role in drafting this document. Eleanor Roosevelt, the wife of the recently deceased President of the US, was the chairperson of the diverse committee. The UN member nations signed and adopted it in 1948. Oh, well…

I volunteered with the American Friends Service Committee of the Pacific, based in San Francisco. Generally helping in any way I could, I particularly focused on their efforts to abolish capital punishment in California. We valiantly tried to remove the US from the shameful group of countries with the highest government murder rates, like China, Iran, Saudi Arabia, and Egypt. That was a fight we could never win.

Executions have never deterred crime and never have. They are done because 'someone must pay', often not the one who actually did the murder, the driver, for example. Let us not mention the completely innocent who are executed by mistake. Every major religious group in the US, including all non-Christian groups, has publicly opposed it as official dogma. The only exception that wholeheartedly supports it is the Southern Baptists; the largest Protestant denomination, mostly comprising fundamentalist evangelicals. Of course, their savior was executed by the Roman government. That fact never gave them pause for thought. Of course, without his execution, where would the Christian Church be today?

The majority of voters always support it. In Europe, every referendum to abolish it failed. Finally, the governments simply abolished it without consulting the voters. The last public execution in the US was in Kentucky in 1936. Over 20,000 spectators came to be entertained. The last public execution in France occurred in 1939. In both cases, the crazy, ugly behavior of the spectators convinced both countries to end public executions. The Taliban still fill sports stadiums with thousands to watch the condemned being stoned to death. Many state governments in the US have quietly stopped the practice without trying to abolish the law. They know it would be a nearly impossible task. Probably the most winning political statement is to be 'tough on crime'.

I volunteered in every other way that I could. I helped a retired man who lived a few blocks from me. He had turned the ground floor of his house into a large distribution space for food. He received surplus food from the Commodity Credit Corporation of the Department of Agriculture. This was food such as dairy and other agricultural products (rice, beans, etc.) that the government bought from farmers to support the market price for them.

He collected surplus food from restaurants and supermarkets as well, and then divided all of this into bags for distribution on Friday mornings to the poor and destitute. I helped him with all this activity.

On Friday mornings, a long line of older Vietnamese women stood waiting to collect the free food, thinking what a wonderful country the US is where one can eat for free.

Another example is I became trained as a California State mediator. This was a program to help neighbors (usually) resolve their conflicts without going to the civil courts. Some conflicts were legitimate, like too much noise late at night. Others were silly, like a neighbor's cat entering their yard. In that case, the cat willfully ignored the sign posted in the yard, written in large letters: "Cats Stay Out!".

Mediation is a process where each side hears the other's point of view, including how that makes them feel. Sometimes it can take many hours, but in the end, they agree on a solution and part not as friends, but at least as neighbors who have a better understanding of how their actions affect others. It is much better than either a court ruling or arbitration, where a superior entity decides the case for them. In mediation, they resolve the case themselves. These solutions are always better and longer lasting than any imposed by outsiders.

Before I was a published author, I had been a poet from an early age. I participated in many poetry readings throughout the San Francisco Bay Area. I read many of my poems. The audience always gave me a warm reception. I joined the San Francisco Bay Poet's Union. Besides publishing our poems in a regular journal, we often planned to go on strike and not write any more poetry until we were better paid. After all, how could a society function without its poets?

I participated in poetry competitions. The Oakland Public Library sponsored one. We had to write a poem about California within two hours with no preparation. My poem won first place and is hanging on the library's walls. I have included the poem at the end for those curious.

Reading was extremely important to me then and now. Every year, the large public libraries had a huge sale of books they no longer needed. These libraries included the ones in Berkeley, Oakland, and San Francisco. One could choose from thousands of books and buy them by the paper shopping bag full for a dollar.

Comparative mythology was my main intellectual pursuit then. Joseph Campbell, Carl Jung, etc. were major influences. I took it so seriously that I applied and was accepted to the University of California, Berkely Comparative Literature Doctorate Program. Comparative Mythology was not yet an academic program, so Comparative Literature was the closest I could find.

Unfortunately, many, if not most, professors of such liberal arts and social 'sciences' programs saw life through glasses that only had the two lenses of Freud and Marx. I experienced this every time we discussed an assigned book or essay in class.

I remember we were discussing Joseph Conrad's story, Typhoon. He is one of my favorite authors. I have read everything he has published. The topic of the discussion was explaining the plot from a Marxist point of view. As the professor started professing his views to start the discussion, all my classmates were dutifully taking notes of everything he said. As for me, I laid my pen on the table and could not believe my ears.

They were all twenty-two and just out of college with their Bachelor of Arts degrees in English Literature and the like. I was in my mid-thirties and had traveled around the world twice, while living and working professionally in foreign lands for over ten years. I had experienced life to a much higher degree than any of my classmates and my professors, too.

After a semester, I quit the program for all the reasons above. Considering how difficult it was to find teaching positions in such a narrow specialty, I could see myself afterwards teaching Greek Mythology to freshmen at some Midwestern college every semester until I retired. I still had too much living to do to end my life like that. I still have, even now.

As one could probably guess by the progression of this experience, I was starting to search for something else to do. Dedicating my life to the service of others was a lofty ideal. However, the stress of teaching the tougher classes in Oakland's public schools was getting to me. The frustrating hopelessness of trying to help the homeless and abolish the death penalty was causing me to look elsewhere for my next path in life.

People ask me if I did it to take a break from my career. I did not intend it to be a break but rather a new path in life. I guess the simple answer is I was too weak to continue, unlike many others who dedicate their whole lives to service to others. At least, I tried for over five years.

I applied to work on a project in Ukraine for the United States Agency for International Aid (USAID). This agency manages all the international non-military projects funded by the US Congress. This project was to help companies in Ukraine, independent for only seven years after the collapse of the Soviet Union, to adapt from a command economy to a free market.

Under the Soviet Union, it was common for a company to have one supplier and one customer. For example, a manufacturing company in Ukraine might have a single supplier of raw materials in Siberia and send all its production to a company in Poland. After the collapse, the Ukrainian company had better options than the Siberian supplier. Likewise, the Polish company no longer wanted anything from Ukraine.

USAID accepted me and sent me to Mykolaiv, a city to the east of Odessa on the Black Sea. It was the major shipbuilding city under the Soviet Union. Now their specialty is nuclear powered icebreakers, among other things. I had to teach a local company how to source suppliers and then how to find and sell to new customers.

I wanted to be prepared before I went. So, I bought every book I could find about Ukraine at the Oakland Public Library's used bookstore. As I prepared to pay, the woman working there said to me that it appeared I was going to Ukraine soon. I replied that indeed I was going there to work on a USAID project.

She explained that she was a Russian who had married an American from the US many years before. Being a product of the Soviet Union; she knew Ukrainians well. She warned me emphatically that I should make sure I did not fall in love with a Ukrainian. They were famous for having a nasty temper and made for bad mates. Did I listen to her? My dear readers will have to read the next chapter to find out.

Me Getting Older

A Life Gone By

Sitting, brooding in a shadow saloon
With a cigar blotting smells of old age.
Hand on my watch, ticking the timeless tune.
An old book, my life has reached the last page.

Dried eyes greet the blur of ghosts as they pass.
Hollow ears catch spirits in the old oaks.
A mind not present, cold as tarnished brass.
The slow silent Companion, my breath cloaks.

A cold violent passage around the Horn,
Made my first fortune in the Fields of Gold.
Cheated by partners, from me my stake torn.
Now here, too late to heed what I was told.

Many years of scorching sun creased my brow.
Heat withered away my dreams on the vine.
To the bank a deed, to my land a bow.
For others will try to turn dust to wine.

Worked on the railroad 'til the Chinese came.
They worked harder and for much less than I.
Walked to the Nevada mines, found some fame.
Returned penniless, with no tears to cry.

Oakland saloon, I opened on credit.
I would stand all day, my foot on the bar
Lives, loves, lessons learned only to forget
Recounted to any from near or far.

Now I sit and stare, finally silent.
Listening for stories of happy times.
Yet, I never hear any; the content
Are not here. They stayed East counting their dimes.

February 2nd, 1997

Poetry and the Visual Arts

The Camera's Voice

First Prize

An Oakland Poetry Competition held at the Oakland Main Library

1999

Ukraine, Bulgaria, Romania, Moldova

Ukraine 1999

A Country in Freefall

After a few stops from San Francisco Airport, I arrived at the Odessa Airport late in the day. Because the roads in the Soviet Union were generally terrible and only became worse after it broke apart, the 134 kilometers/83 miles trip to my destination of Mykolaiv took over three hours. We went straight to a restaurant for dinner, where most of the key employees of the company were waiting.

USAID sent them my resume before I arrived, so they knew at least my background. As is normal, I included a few of my non-professional activities with certificates and diplomas, etc. One of the many things I did before was to join Toastmasters, the international public speaking organization. I even joined a Mandarin speaking group in San Francisco's Chinatown. Never having had a problem speaking in public, I progressed to the top of the various levels. I included this achievement.

Of all the things on my resume, one thing stood out for them: I was a Toastmaster. Clearly, they understood it very differently from what I knew. There is a strong tradition in Georgia of giving long and poetic toasts before everyone throws back their vodka. Since I somehow gained this wonderful oratory skill living in California, they constantly urged me to make such toasts to everyone. I tried, and though being a poet, I could never quite get it right, despite my beautiful interpreter's efforts. After many, many attempts and the combination of jetlag, I had to surrender. I learned their understanding of my master toasting skills later. In the meantime, they had to deliver me to my bed.

My USAID sponsors warned me not to try to keep up with the Ukrainians when drinking vodka. Rather than heed this warning, I took it as a challenge. I was born and raised in a time when it was considered a manly virtue to be able to drink more than anyone else. We were whiskey drinkers, mainly. And we of the Northeast drank our whiskey 'neat' with nothing else in it, not like the Southerners who mix their whiskey with a glass of Coke and ice. The horror!

Because of this, I always impressed my fellow Ukrainian drinkers. The people of that part of the world, almost always men, would hold a shot glass of vodka in one hand and something pickled in the other hand to serve as a chaser. Immediately after downing the vodka, they would chase it with the pickled thing. Often it was either a pickled mushroom, cucumber, onion, or even a small smoked Baltic fish. I never did that part of the ritual, much to their amazement and respect.

My interpreter's full-time job was as an interpreter at one of the large shipyards the city is famous for. Since they had trouble paying her, she was free to take on part-time jobs here and there, like interpreting for me. She had the classical beauty of Slavic women, whom I think are the most physically beautiful women in the world. There is a reason why artistic gymnastics is my favorite Olympic sport. The sport is dominated by Slavic goddesses from Ukraine, Russia, Belarus, and Poland. If they were to compete nude, billions of men would watch it across the globe.

Ironically, she was a part of the great Soviet sports machine, exactly in artistic gymnastics. Children around six years old were identified as having potential in one sport or another. They were inducted into the machine at that point. They were taken from their parents to train and live at special schools far from home. Their parents could visit them only twice a year. They trained for most of the day, with a few hours left over for academics.

Of course, most could not take the hundred percent dedication to their sport and snapped before dropping out along the way for not being mentally strong enough. My interpreter lasted until her high school years. Then they returned to the normal education system as failures. Those who do manage to get through to age eighteen might still fail the national competitions that chose only the best. They are not qualified to enter university, so they become physical education teachers in the school system as another cog in the sports machine.

Since winning is everything, illegal sports doping was rampant and normal practice, even now. Old addictions are hard to kick. Obviously, this system produced a large population of mentally and emotionally, and even physically, scarred people. Why would a country do that? Is winning sports trophies so important? The answer is yes. In the world of socialism, nothing is more important than international prestige, their standing vis-à-vis their non-socialist competitors.

Ukraine and the rest of the ex-Soviet countries were all in free fall in the years after independence. Economic and social collapse was still in full force when I arrived. The entire Soviet world of seventy-five years was demolished. Oligarchs were in full control. These were various Communist Party chiefs who found themselves in positions of power and great wealth purely by luck.

Everything in the Soviet Union was owned by the People. This included every factory, every mine, everything. The workers were given pieces of paper to represent their fractional ownership of the place where they worked. Since there was no stock market, they had no way to turn it into anything of value. They sold their shares for a bottle of vodka and a loaf of bread. Those with enough ruthless imagination and stolen money could create enormous empires of wealth and power.

That is how the owners of all the great contemporary companies in this vast area of the globe came to their immense wealth. Communist Party thieves stole the property of the People. It is that simple. Anyone rich in these countries gained their wealth this way. There is very little besides natural resources and weapons that these countries produce (except computer games and a PC security program that has now been banned by most companies in the West).

However, at the local level, there were small players who became entrepreneurs and gave something positive to their local economies. Dimitri, the owner of the company USAID tasked me to help, was one of these. He had the foresight to understand that people now owned their apartments and houses. They would want to personalize them from the days of collective ownership under socialism. He built his company on providing interior design and all the things required to turn that dream into reality, including furniture, fittings, lighting, flooring — in short, everything.

He also had other businesses, such as sausage production (yes, I have seen how sausages are made) and construction materials like concrete and flagstones. My project was to help him succeed even more. Besides my very attractive interpreter, I had an affable young man about my age who spoke decent English. His job was a 'marketer' in a country that had no idea what that was. In practice, he was my handler, who was supposed to keep me out of danger in the chaotic and perilous world of the post-Soviet Union.

Dimitri gave me an apartment to stay in. It was small because a wall divided it into two halves. As was very common at that time, people slept on sofa beds, turning their living rooms into bedrooms by pulling open their sofas. His mother owned it.

My interpreter's family consisted of her parents and a younger brother. Her father was the head of the trade union at one of the three huge shipyards there. The State gave him a small one-bedroom apartment that they shared with their Rottweiler, who was the size of another person. She slept in the only bedroom. Her brother slept on a reclining chair in the living room, while her parents slept on a divan in the back of the same room.

Her mother worked as an accountant at a brewery. Besides her full-time job, she made a full breakfast for her family. She did the same for lunch and dinner, when everyone came home for both. In addition, she took care of all the housework. She had no washing machines for clothes or dishes. They had no hot water either. A shower meant standing in the bathtub with a bucket of boiled water from the stove and mixing it with the cold water from the tap. She hung the clothes to dry on the balcony, where they froze into stiff boards in the winter, flapping in the icy wind. This had not changed since the days of the Soviet Union, as I wrote in that chapter.

Dimitri was an excellent example of an entrepreneur in the early days of the post-Soviet system. He created fifty or more jobs. This alone made him a hero of Ukraine, with its very high unemployment rate. He did not receive a badge of honor, as all heroes of the Soviet Union did. Then, as an entrepreneur, he would have been considered a criminal. The Soviet Union awarded my interpreter's mother a medal of Heroine of the Soviet Union because she had two children. What would that have made my mother, who had six? A socialist goddess?

Before I arrived, I bought a bottle of good tequila at the airport in Frankfurt. My handler and I shared a small glass on the apartment balcony after work. Since I knew he had only ever experienced cheap vodka, I knew this would be a treat, and indeed it was. I will never forget the sorrow on his face when we finally finished it weeks later, despite having carefully rationed it.

I could walk to the office in about fifteen minutes. It always amused me when people, thinking I was a local, often stopped to ask me the time. Then I realized I was the only one wearing a wristwatch. Sometimes people stopped to ask me for directions. In those cases, I pretended to be mute. They would apologize before hurrying away. It was best to hide the fact that I was a foreigner in those lawless days.

The Soviet Union had an intricate network of barter trade with its friends and allies. They traded goods rather than paid with money. No one wanted their worthless currencies, and they lacked the hard currencies to spare like US dollars, Swiss francs, or British pounds, etc. I experienced it when I was working in Hong Kong for a Swiss company and organized barter trade between Yugoslavia and Asian consumer goods suppliers. In this case, the Swiss paid the Asian suppliers in francs, and the Yugoslavs repaid the Swiss with construction materials to sell in Western Europe.

This business would not have happened if the Swiss had not been the middlemen. With no such middlemen with hard currency, the system required experts in all the participating countries. They knew at any given moment how many Cuban Cohiba cigars were worth a container of spare parts for their sugar processing equipment. How many Syrian oranges equaled how many barrels of oil? How many tons of rice equaled fighter jet spare parts? The possibilities were endless.

This system continues to now. I had a Cohiba cigar after dinner in a wonderful restaurant in Odessa for the equivalent of one US dollar. I bought them in China for about the same price. Dimitri had two barter experts with their own office in his company. Their barter trades could include many steps in between. Country A has Z available and needs M. Country B has Y available and needs N. Country C has X available and needs Z. Country D has N available and needs X, etc. Somewhere in between all of that, Dimitri can trade what he has for what he needs. They may need to go through several transactions to complete it. Trade M for X so he can trade X for N so he can trade N for Y so that he has Y to trade for the hardwood to make the quality floors for his clients.

This concept of barter operated with domestic workers, too. One day while I was working in the office, a large truck full of plums parked in front of the company offices at the end of the workday. Dimitri was paying his employees in part with kilograms of plums, which they would have to sell in the market on the weekend. Once my interpreter's mother had to do repairs on their home. She paid the repairmen half in cash and half in vodka (after the work was done).

Though Dimitri had a fairly complex business, he made all the decisions himself. There was always a long line of employees outside his office requiring his decision regarding something quite petty in most cases. A typical example was requiring his approval to buy more toilet paper or more pens. (What? Already?). I imagined that is how a Mafia Don's office would operate.

His heart was not in the best shape despite only being in his forties. One can tell when people have weak hearts because they are always leaning on something like the edge of a table, a chair, the wall, etc. while they are standing. I advised him to reduce the stress by letting his employees make lower-level decisions on their own. His response was, "What if they make a wrong decision?" I had to train him in the general management of employees.

Restaurant menus were always very interesting. They continued the old Soviet tradition of putting the weights of all the ingredients below every item on the menu. A patron knew exactly how many grams of olives, feta cheese, etc. were in his Greek salad. I never saw anyone bring small scales to weigh them. To make a phone call (only landlines) one had to first dial one's own phone number before dialing the other party's phone number. Otherwise, how would the phone company know whom to charge?

Once while walking through the city center, much to my surprise, I met a Chinese man there. We started talking. I asked him how he had ended up there and what he was doing. He met an attractive local woman, married her, and had a few children. He was doing some small business that the Chinese are so adept at doing wherever they are.

I named Ukraine 'the land of the lotus eaters'. This refers to the story in the Odyssey when Odysseus and his men arrive at an island where they ate the local specialty of the intoxicating lotus plant. Afterwards, they completely forgot about returning home. He partook of the lotus. I did too, but the lotus wanted to leave with me.

The beauty of Ukrainian women could certainly make one so blissful as to be blind to the complete disaster a country in freefall would be. Anything of value was stolen. Brass statues in public parks disappeared in the middle of the night. Once while I was there, in the middle of the day, a team of thieves dressed as telephone company employees used a company truck and stole hundreds of meters of telephone lines from the poles along the street for the copper in them.

Walking up apartment stairs at night was hazardous as the lightbulbs were all stolen. No one dared to use the elevators. I hired a driver to take me out to the nearby vineyards in his old BMW. I was sitting in the back seat with both windows shut. It was hot. Using the air conditioning was out of the question. When I went to unroll the window, there was no crank handle to do so. I asked him about that. He handed me one, but then after opening the window, I had to immediately return it. He had taken a few Russians on a recent tour, and they stole both.

Much of this petty crime occurred during the Soviet Union, too. When one parked one's car, one always had to take off the windshield wipers and hide them inside the car. For example, if one parked outside the open market without doing so, one would most likely see the same windshield wipers for sale by an enterprising entrepreneur.

During my wanderings throughout the city, I met a third generation Ukriano-Canadian. He decided to go to the newly independent home of his forbearers and help the best he could. There was a reasonably well-appointed bar and restaurant in a great location. He bought it from the city and invested quite a sum in turning the quasi-ruin into a place of nearly Western standards. The local politicos liked what he did with it and coveted it for themselves. They confiscated it, simply stole it without paying him anything. He was still there, trying to fight to get it back when I met him. For this and many more reasons, I would never do business in that part of the world.

There was a row of bars and restaurants beside the large plaza by the river. I enjoyed going to them after work. I was surprised at how good some of the Ukrainian and Russian beer was. It was very pleasant to drink a few bottles while sitting outside. Unfortunately, just on the other side of the low wall separating the outdoor sitting area from the street was a row of half a dozen boys of about ten years old and one elderly man waiting for me to leave so they could grab the empty bottles to sell them for a pittance. When I left, I gave the elderly man the few bottles I had, much to the chagrin of the boys.

Mykolaiv is a delightful city. It has an excellent art museum filled with wonderful seascapes painted by local painters in the 1800's. I doubt anyone can capture the grace of a crashing wave like they could. The beauty of Odessa is even greater with its Opera House and the so-called Potemkin Stairs, named after the famous scene in Eisenstein's 1925 movie, The Battleship Potemkin. After Catherine the Great conquered southern Ukraine from the Ottoman's she built a port on the Black Sea and brought in Italian and French architects to design the charming city that we know today.

The company threw a party for me on my last day. Afterwards, my handler, who became my buddy, took me to his favorite places in Mykolaiv. I had quite a bit more vodka, but unfortunately not enough. I wrote 'unfortunately' because I could remember everything that happened later.

When it was time for me to return to my flat, he walked with me to make sure nothing happened. Nothing would have happened, except that we met the local police. I was carrying a briefcase that only had a bottle of champagne that Dimitri gave me and a cheap camera. I was smart enough to keep everything of value in his office safe. They took a strong interest in that, probably thinking it was filled with unmarked hundred-dollar bills. My buddy said something about leaving me alone. That response brought out their clubs. They beat him badly, cutting his face up. I went down with just one hit to the head.

I woke up on the floor shirtless, where they had thrown me, in a dirty jail cell. Dimitri managed to get me out by late morning. I will never know how much he paid or the strings he pulled. I suppose it was not illegal to walk with a briefcase. Being a US citizen might have helped. They returned my destroyed briefcase (I must have locked it) with my camera but minus the champagne. When I returned to California and developed the film, I found they had taken many photos of me lying on the jail floor. How lovely. Despite that, I was still young enough to bounce back. After cleaning myself up with a change of clothes, I left for Bulgaria later that day with my interpreter.

An Old Lada in front of an Older House

Bulgaria, Romania, Moldova 1999

Where Are the Restaurants?

After my Mykolaiv project ended, I took some time to visit the region with my interpreter. I invited her to go with me not because I needed an interpreter, but because she was a very attractive woman who showed a warm interest in me. We took a long-distance bus that lasted most of the day from Odesa to Varna, a beautiful ancient Greek colony on Bulgaria's Black Sea coast.

At that time, it was still a Soviet era resort with a charming old town and Soviet-era hotels along the coast. Today, it is a thriving tourist town overrun by Westerners. We stayed at one such Cold War hotel. We had to climb down steep steps to the narrow beach below. Freighters used the nearby port, so the water was not clean enough for swimming. As we walked among the rocks and the dark sand, we passed an impromptu nudist beach. As with most nudist beaches around the world, the nudists were mostly middle-aged gay men.

We had dinner with an acquaintance of hers. He shared with me the typical Eastern European prejudice against gypsies, explaining to me that all crime in Bulgaria is caused by them. I asked a clarifying question by repeating what he had said. "ALL crime in Bulgaria is done by gypsies? Really?" Giving him a chance to backpedal on his sweeping statement. But no, he powered forward by affirming that indeed they do.

Romania, 1999: After a few days in Varna, we continued by bus to Bucharest, the capital of Romania, about a four-hour bus ride north. My first memory is of a large, speeding horse cart that nearly ran me over when I tried to cross the main road outside the bus station. I was surprised to see horse carts still being a primary means of commercial transport. It was not to be my only surprise in Romania's largest city.

After thanking me in the best way she knew how in my hotel room, she took the train to Odesa and back to work in the shipyard. I was on my own to explore Romania. After a typical holiday in Varna, I was ready to travel the way I normally do, open to any adventurous experience that would come my way.

Bucharest was not a particularly attractive city. What struck me most saliently about the city was the almost total lack of restaurants. I had to walk far and wide to find any. One afternoon I stumbled onto the national ethnic village, which had a restaurant serving traditional Romanian fare. I always enjoy these open-air museums of different traditional architecture examples from various regions around the country, as I have seen in other countries during my travels.

There was not much to do in the evenings. I had moved from a hotel to a guesthouse for the few backpackers visiting Romania. So, to amuse myself, in the morning I would buy a half a liter bottle of Țuică (pronounced suiker), the national drink of Romania, and put it in the freezer to consume later that evening. Țuică is traditionally made of plums, but other types of fruit are also used. It is similar in taste and strength to German schnaps.

Another thing that I found interesting is that Romanian is a Romance language, which is even more incredible considering they are surrounded by Slavic speaking people. I can read their newspapers and understand the main gist. We can thank the Romans for this. They named their eastern province Dacia, which is the name of Romania's car brand exported throughout Europe.

My next destination was Moldova, a small country between Ukraine and Romania. It was on the way to Odesa, where I would fly back to California. While I was still in Bucharest, I called the Moldovan embassy to learn how to get a visa. No one at the embassy spoke English. I had to use my old backup, French, which worked well.

During the Soviet era, learning English was frowned upon as it was the language of the US and its various capitalist running dogs (to borrow a Chinese Communist Party description), the principal adversary of socialism everywhere. French, however, was encouraged, being the language of very left-leaning France with its thinly disguised anti-US sentiment of the time. I learned French because it was the language of Camus, Sartre, Rousseau, Voltaire, and Arsène Lupin.

After a few days in Bucharest, it was time for me to explore more of the country. I took the train to Suceava in the northeast, near Ukraine, in the heart of the wonderful region of the Bucovina church murals. These vibrantly colorful and well-preserved UNESCO murals cover both the exterior and interior walls of these ancient churches that were part of the local monasteries built in the fifteenth and sixteenth centuries. The Voronet Monastery is probably the best example.

It would have been impossible to visit them by public transportation, as the half dozen of the best examples are spread across the region and in the deep countryside. I considered renting a car from a car rental office I saw near my hotel. As luck would have it, I met a young man hanging around the outside.

He spoke good English and offered to drive me to all the sites for the whole day in his car. He charged me fifty US dollars for everything, which was very reasonable considering what renting a car for the day would have cost. I also did not relish the idea of driving in the Romanian deep country trying to find my way from one monastery to the next.

Because of him, I was able to spend a very pleasant day with a pleasant Romanian, accomplishing my goal in Bucovina. We stopped for lunch at a farmer's restaurant, which offered an excellent opportunity to experience traditional Romanian cuisine. I paid for lunch, and he had the chance to speak English all day while earning about a week's wage. It was a win-win all round.

My next stop was Iasi, a major city close to Moldova. Early in the morning, I walked to the train station and bought my ticket. As there was no English (or French) anywhere, I could not be sure on which platform the train would be. I boarded the train that I thought was correct, according to the ticket seller's mimed instructions. To be sure, I asked the man sitting across from me if this was the train to Iasi. He spoke no English, so I just repeated Iasi while pointing to the train's floor. He shook his head and motioned me to another train. And so started another adventure.

I shared the train compartment with Romania's first baseball team. The players were between ten and fourteen years old, which would put them in the Little League if they were in the US. Their Romanian coach spoke good English and explained how such a strange thing came to be.

The US ambassador to Romania donated all the paraphernalia to fit out a Little League baseball team, including bats, balls, gloves, etc. The coach only had seven boys to fill out a normal nine-player team, but he had to start somewhere. They were traveling to compete with another such team somewhere else in Romania.

The train to Iasi is only about three hours. Five hours later, I was starting to wonder. My doubts were answered when the train conductor came by checking tickets. She was a no-nonsense woman in her thirties and definitely in charge. A few lackeys trailed her as she made her way down the train corridor.

Though she spoke no English, I understood her request and dutifully handed my ticket to Iasi to her. This created quite a scandal, and her reaction proved it. Luckily, the English-speaking baseball coach sitting beside me could interpret. As I suspected by then, the man on the correct train at the Suceava station directed me to the wrong one. I will never know if I was seriously mispronouncing the word 'Iasi' or if he did it out of spite or fun, as I suspect. But there I was on a train going in the opposite direction, deep into Transylvania.

In such situations, early on I learned that we just need to roll with whatever life throws at us. There is no other choice. And so, I did. I told her I was very sorry for any inconvenience and that I would get off at the next station and change to the correct train. Her angry response made it clear she was not having any of that. She wanted to prosecute me to the fullest extent of the law.

She demanded that I give her my passport. This I refused to do. The only time a uniformed representative of a country can take one's passport is when they are proceeding with deportation. I told her that, and she backed off. So, we agreed I would do as I suggested and get off at the next station. She walked off in a huff to check the tickets of the next compartment.

The train continued for another half hour. Meanwhile, I enjoyed the scenery, which had turned from hills and valleys into heavily forested mountains. It was also the fabled home of the famous Count Dracula, also known as Prince Vlad III, the Impaler. Though I was hopeful not to be impaled for my grand crime, I could not be sure if somehow his spirit was not lurking about.

When the train arrived at the station of a large town in the heart of Transylvania, she got off with me and took me to the ticket window to make sure I bought the correct ticket for the correct train, which was leaving many hours later. Then, something extraordinary happened. Her train continued its journey. But she stayed behind with me.

She motioned that we should walk into the center of town. She spoke no English, and I spoke no Romanian. What was left? I tried French. She managed to pull that out of her high school past. It was a struggle. As we passed a bookstore, I bought her a French-Romanian-French dictionary. When communication stalled, I could look up the word in French and show her the Romanian word, and vice versa.

It was lunchtime, and my day had an early start. We went to a grand restaurant in the center. Now, knowing her intentions were friendly, I treated her to lunch and was ready for whatever came next. She showed me around town, which turned out to be where she lived. She took me to the local woodworking museum. Meanwhile, the whole time she was wearing her gray conductor's uniform.

All too soon the hour of the Isai train approached. I told her I had better return to the train station. She told me not to worry about the train. My trip to Iasi could wait. I noticed that there were a few hotels nearby. I suggested we go to one. She knew what I meant but demurred without rejecting the idea out of hand. She was so different from our first encounter on the train; I wondered if she was back on her medication.

We went to her favorite café/bar, where we spent some agreeable hours in the pleasant garden having drinks and snacks, while conversing the best we could. We had dinner, and as the witching hour drew near; I was becoming curious how my day would end. At the very least, I needed a place to sleep to be ready to sort out the following day. I still had no idea what she was thinking.

She suggested that I could sleep at her place. That would work, I thought. So, we walked to a small house surrounded by a garden in the suburbs. Turns out she was living with her parents, who were warmly welcoming. Her mother made a quick, traditional Romanian dinner of fried potatoes and other things. I had more surprises coming.

As we were sitting at the kitchen table, a young man entered. It was her husband! Their baby was asleep in another room. Despite his friendly greeting, I could tell he was as perplexed by the situation as I was. It was around midnight. She had to catch the first train the next morning — ironically, the one to Iasi. We would need to leave the house shortly after 0600. It was a long and strange day. I needed to go to sleep.

As I stretched out on the sofa puzzling over the events of the day, I did not know if she would visit me in the middle of the night or he would with a knife. It turned out neither one did. The next morning, we left at the crack of dawn and walked to the station in the darkness, me with my backpack and her in her gray uniform. She led me to the compartment where the train conductor and colleagues would sit. Everyone was quite friendly and accepting of the unusual situation.

Every time the train arrived at a station, and the train staff had to leave and do their jobs, she would lock me in. I do not know what she was thinking. Perhaps she thought I would try to escape and get off at the wrong station. Finally, the train arrived at Iasi. She got off with me. She put a piece of paper with her address into my hand, kissed me on my lips, then boarded the train with a smile. I walked into town, shaking my head.

Before continuing to Chisinau, the capital of Moldova, my last stop on my trip before returning to Odesa, I spent a few days in the city of Iasi. It was quite an adventure getting there. I figured I had better at least see the place.

Iasi is the third largest city in Romania and the regional capital of Moldavia. It is located close to the Moldovan border. Besides the various imposing buildings built in a long-lost time several wars before, what I remember most about the city were the large groups of gypsy women. Their vibrantly colorful dresses added much needed color to an otherwise drab city.

Moldova 1999: Moldova, sometimes called Bessarabia, has a complicated history. To simplify, it was once part of the Ottoman and then the Russian empires. Later, it became part of Romania before the Soviet empire annexed it after the Second World War. After the Soviet Union's collapse in 1991, Moldova, which was one of the Soviet Socialist Republics, declared independence.

There remains a long, thin strip of land on the eastern bank of the Dniester River that remains as part of post-Soviet Russia. Russian troops are stationed there to prevent any Moldovan attempt to retake their lost land. The majority of Moldova are really of ethnic Romanian origin. You would think they would want to return to their people and reunify with Romania. There are two reasons why that has not happened.

The first is the Soviet collapse hit Moldova particularly hard. The economy is in terrible condition. Romania probably does not have the resources required to raise Moldova to a level anywhere near where Romania is, not to mention the minimum standards that the European Union would require. The second reason is that, as bad as Moldova is, the local leaders probably do not want to give up their power. They probably follow the Chinese adage that it is better to be the head of a chicken than the tail of a tiger.

Chisinau has many examples of Francophile architecture built between the World Wars in the 1920's and 1930's. Romania traditionally was a great admirer of France and had hoped to sign a defense alliance with them against the rising tide of fascism. Being too far from France to offer any real help, the French refused. The King of Romania then was Carlos II. The Romanian fascists forced him into exile in 1940 so they could align their country with Nazi Germany. Despite his Prussian roots, King Carlos hated the Nazis.

His family was unemployed Prussian nobility when Romania won its independence in 1877. As with many newly independent European states, rather than joining the modern world and creating democratic republics, they opted to create anachronistic monarchies with foreign noble families. King Carlos exiled himself to Portugal. Ironically, I lived in his palace in Estoril, where he had lived from 1940 until he died in 1953.

The city has many examples of surprising architecture, like a smaller version of the Arc de Triumph. Wandering through the city, I could not help but notice the similarities with neighboring Ukraine, with its obvious Soviet mark.

Moldova was famous in the Soviet Union for being the primary source of sparkling wine. No celebration could be without it. The Russians of the 1800's put champagne on the world map of major wine production. After Napoleon was finally defeated at Waterloo, the victorious Russian army occupied Paris. There, the officers discovered the sweet, bubbly wine. They became great fans and imported it by the millions of bottles after they returned to Russia.

Champagne was not popular before that. We can see that from the statistics. In 1800, 300,000 bottles of champagne were produced. That number ballooned to twenty million by 1850. We can read many examples of these great champagne parties of the rich in the novels of Dostoevsky, Tolstoy, Turgenev, etc. It was the favorite drink of Russian Calvary officers (sons of the aristocracy). Drinking vodka was so low class. But every bottle of vodka was equivalent to four bottles of champagne in terms of alcohol content. One can see how that twenty million bottle number came to be.

Another curious footnote is that the word for bistro has its origins with the same occupying Russian army. They wanted a quick and easy place to eat lunch that mainly consisted of sandwiches made with baguettes. We can find them everywhere today. The word 'bistro' is the Russian word for 'fast'.

I visited many local winery outlets of Moldovan sparkling wine in the city center, though I have never been a fan of anything sparkling, usually skipping it for another substitute during celebrations. I did find a very reasonably priced ornate restaurant, where I could eat like a prince and finish it all off with a bartered Cohiba cigar.

To spend an afternoon, I went to the Opera House, where I saw Rob Roy, an opera based on Walter Scott's novel. The idea of a Walter Scott opera intrigued me, so I bought my ticket and found my seat. Next to me sat an obese, middle-aged Russian woman who had been living in Chisinau since Soviet times. She took an immediate liking to me. Surprisingly, for that part of the world at that time, she spoke reasonable English. She had lived in the UK for a few years.

As we waited for the opera to start, she made it quite clear that she would like to take me back to her place afterwards for dinner and other entertainment. As flattered as I was, I was very noncommittal, preferring women half her size (and age). Nonetheless, I did not want to offend her with an outright refusal, or worse, humiliate her with a laugh.

The conductor entered the stage to much applause. The President of the Republic followed him and gave him an enormous bouquet of flowers. They then hugged and kissed each other on the lips. She was much scandalized by two men kissing in an act of friendship. Since it is a normal greeting between officials and the like in Russia, I did not understand her reaction. As far as I could tell, tongues stayed in their respective mouths.

After some thought, I decided she was feigning outrage for my sake, a Westerner from where most men do not greet each other like that. I shrugged it off. During the confusion of everyone parting at the end, I gave her the slip by ducking into the men's room.

Moldova had sunk even further in every way than both its neighbors. It positively made Ukraine look prosperous. The seediness of the train station area was only superseded by the seediness around the bus station. I was glad to return to gray Odesa by train. I was even more so when my plane landed back in sunny Southern California.

As my readers might have surmised, I did indeed fall in love with my beautiful interpreter against the best advice. Besides having a light on, she was a rare Ukrainian who smiled. I brought her back to California with me. Why that was a terrible idea will be a story for another time.

Ruins Among the Daisies

Postscript

I could have continued for another twenty-six years to bring my story up to date. But I chose to end this account at the end of 1999 for two reasons. The first is that the world changed to be closer to what we experience today. Namely, cell phones, the internet, GPS, etc. have transformed traveling to be much easier and more convenient.

The other main reason is that my life changed greatly, too. I seriously embarked on my career, which took me to the heights of the corporate world in the roles of President and COO for global manufacturing companies. Gone were the days of money worries. I no longer had to stay in guesthouses with a prostitute wing or take uncomfortable long-distance bus trips.

My career took me back to Asia, but also to South America and Europe. I never lost my curiosity and interest in the world. I traveled to forty-six countries between 1983 and 1999. By now, that total is eighty-nine. I once had a life goal of visiting every country in the world. Well, I have slowed down and may not achieve it.

In some ways, I am still that wide eyed twenty-year-old. I have lived and worked for over half my life outside my land of birth in twelve foreign countries. In many other ways, I have become jaded with the world. I no longer need to see every sight there is in a new place. How many churches, mosques, palaces, etc. does one need to visit to get the idea?

My values have not changed. I treat everyone with the dignity we all deserve. I choose to see the humanity rather than the labels of creed and color. Every stranger has something to teach me. I retired at age fifty-three and have chosen Portugal to be my home. I have settled here for the duration, where I write and enjoy whatever life has in store for me next.

Final Thoughts

Thank you very much for reading my story. I trust you enjoyed it. This is the result of many years of work. I ask you, dear reader, to please leave a thoughtful and considerate review on Amazon. These are especially important to authors. Please type the link below into your browser and you will be taken directly to the book page.

http://www.amazon.com/review/create-review?&asin=B0GYLTP9YC

About the Author

Born in Philadelphia, Thomas Murray is foremost a storyteller and has been writing all his life. He is the author of The Eye of the Beholder, The Adventures of Nuno and Figo, Only After Dark, The Amazing Tale of Gwennie, and Ponce de León: A Modern Sequel. He currently lives in Portugal.

Having lived overseas for over twenty-five years on five continents and traveled to eighty-nine countries, he has trained his mind to be sensitive to the wide range of nuances and world views that make up the personalities of everyone he meets. Greatly appreciating global cultures, he includes many details about the places and characters to make readers feel they are part of the story. When he is not writing, he is traveling and learning foreign languages, currently Portuguese.

You can learn more about Thomas and his writing at

www.thomasmurraywriter.com

Please like his Facebook page: www.facebook.com/thmurraywriter

You can contact the writer at Bastet Publishing: info@bastet.ink

Other Books by the Same Author

The Eye of the Beholder: International Suspense in the Art World, Bastet Publishing, 2020 (first in the Gwendolyn series)

A young art forger on the run …

Gwendolyn, a likable rogue with attitude, is secretly a successful fine-art forger, rubbing shoulders with society's elite and shady art dealers. When she switches her painting with the original in a private home and escapes, she is confident with another successful heist. Until the next day, when the owners are found murdered.

Framed for murder, she must travel to dangerous, exotic lands to find the real murderers and clear her name. But as she delves deeper into the dangerous underworld of art forgery and betrayal, she realizes that she may be in over her head.

As the stakes get higher and her enemies close in, Gwendolyn must use all her cunning and skill to survive. Will she be able to untangle the web of lies and clear her name? Or will she become the next victim in a deadly game of cat and mouse?

https://www.amazon.es/dp/1735260606

Red Is a Color: International Suspense in the Art World, Bastet Publishing, 2024 (second in the Gwendolyn series)

Is it a crime to be a redhead?

Gwendolyn, our favorite art forger and seductress extraordinaire, returns for another hair-raising adventure. Set in the sensuous backdrop of Portugal, Gwendolyn's latest project starts off as just another painting to forge and another wealthy eccentric to con. But as she delves deeper into the lifestyle of her unsuspecting mark, she uncovers more questions than answers.

How did he acquire a previously unknown Renaissance masterpiece by Botticelli? Why does he spend every evening worshipfully gazing at his personal goddess of love? Who is his tempestuous friend with an evil obsession with redheads? Who are the fanatical cultists trailing her every move?

The shadows of reality and myth blur, threatening to swallow her up in a deadly abyss… Will she survive this latest escapade with her life, much less her sanity intact?

www.amazon.com/dp/B0D64LM15C

The Adventures of Nuno and Figo: An Illustrated Journey of Two Unlikely Friends, Bastet Publishing, 2020 (first in the Gwennie series)

One clever rat, one tramp steamship, one hungry lynx …

Experience an adventure unlike any other. Follow Nuno, a clever Iberian Lynx, as he embarks on a treacherous journey to Southern California in search of a new life. Along the way, he meets Figo, a streetwise ship rat, who introduces him to the different cultures, music, and cuisines of the ports they visit.

Together, they face perils lurking around every corner as they form an unlikely friendship. Will it endure the journey, or will the dangers of California prove too difficult to survive? With beautiful illustrations by Madalena Bastos, this is a book you won't want to miss. The author will donate 10% of net proceeds to one or several organizations whose mission is to save the wonderful Iberian Lynx.

https://www.amazon.es/dp/1735260622

The Amazing Tale of Gwennie: Homeless to Palace, Bastet Publishing, 2022 (second and last in the Gwennie series)

From homeless cat to palace queen…

How did Gwennie journey from being a forlorn, homeless cat in southern California to being the spoiled queen of a palace in Portugal? As the daughter of Nuno, an Iberian Lynx, and Terpsie, a Maine Coon cat, this (mostly) true story continues as the second in the series that started with The Adventures of Nuno and Figo: The Incredible Journey of Two Unlikely Friends (Illustrated). Gwennie travels to even more exotic places than her famous father. Follow her journey as she incredibly ends up in Portugal, the same country as her father's homeland, a half a world away.

https://www.amazon.es/dp/B0BCS7NNBX

Only After Dark: One Man's Descent into Obsession and Madness, Bastet Publishing, 2021

Prepare to be enthralled by a dark and beguiling world as an American author of horror discovers an alluring and mysterious existence beyond his own in post-Revolution Portugal of the late 1970s. Running from his past, he moves into an abandoned, crumbling palace, eager to make progress on his next bestselling novel. A chance encounter with an unnamed, yet shockingly sensual woman pulls aside the veil of the world to reveal an alluring existence defined by unnatural delights and mind-twisting hedonism.

As his mysterious lover draws him further into her realm of shadows and ultimate pleasure, how much is he willing to sacrifice to keep her? And will there be anything left of his sanity when his would-be goddess is through with him? A tale told in the vein of Lovecraft and Edgar Allen Poe, this book will have you on the edge of your seat and wanting more.

https://www.amazon.es/dp/1735260673

Ponce de León: A Modern Sequel, Bastet Publishing, 2022

What is the meaning of life if you can live forever?

What if 500 years ago Ponce de León did discover the Fountain of Youth? He and his crew have everything anyone could dream of: wealth, health, the love of friends, and time; eternal time. But is immortality a blessing or a curse? Ponce de Léon is not so sure. He enters a personal crisis seeking this answer to the meaning of life. His search for answers leads him to a truth he never expected.

https://www.amazon.es/dp/173526069X

www.ingramcontent.com/pod-product-compliance
Lightning Source LLC
LaVergne TN
LVHW090558110826
845146LV00001B/174

* 9 7 9 8 9 8 6 5 8 5 6 6 6 *